COMMON HERITAGE

Karachi
Oxford University Press
Oxford   New York   Delhi
1997

Oxford University Press, Walton Street, Oxford OX2 6DP

Oxford   New York
Athens   Auckland   Bangkok   Bombay
Calcutta   Cape Town   Dar es Salaam   Delhi
Florence   Hong Kong   Istanbul   Karachi
Kuala Lumpur   Madras   Madrid   Melbourne
Mexico City   Nairobi   Paris   Singapore
Taipei   Tokyo   Toronto
and associated companies in
Berlin   Ibadan

Oxford is a trade mark of Oxford University Press

© Oxford University Press, 1997

ISBN 0 19 577808 1

Printed in Pakistan at
Challenger Paper Products, Karachi.
Published by
Ameena Saiyid, Oxford University Press
5-Bangalore Town, Sharae Faisal
PO Box 13033, Karachi-75350, Pakistan.

CONTENTS

Muhammad Ali Siddiqui

Muhammad Ali Siddiqui is the Director of the Quaid-i-Azam Academy in Karachi. He is a well-known literary critic and an award-winning writer.

Born in 1938, Dr Siddiqui's professional career has been a peculiar but rich blend of the disciplines of journalism and teaching. This combined with his knowledge of several European and oriental languages has given his writings a particularly novel perspective and a fine and rare cogency.

He has delivered lectures and papers at some of the most prestigious institutes of learning around the world including the School of Oriental and African Studies (SOAS) of the London University, the Oslo University, Norway, as well as several colleges and universities in Canada.

He is a member of several writers associations and guilds based locally as well in other parts of the globe. During the early eighties he was a frequent participant at the various International Urdu Conferences held in Scandinavia and North America. His publications include several books on literary criticism. His award-winning works in Urdu are *Tawazun* and *Croce ki Sargozasht* a translation of Bendetto Croce's autobiography into Urdu.

Introduction

Nostalgia and Much More

The one-thousand-year-long interaction between the Muslims and Hindus in most parts of the subcontinent—and in some areas like Sindh and southern Punjab over 1200 years—produced a peculiar socio-politico-cultural mosaic. The Muslim rulers and Muslim mystics were in competition with each other to give diametrically opposite images of Islam to the Indian masses. While the Hindu-majority areas did not embrace Islam by way of mass conversions, they could not resist imbibing certain features of Muslim culture. The Islamic rule was—save for the Mughal-Rajput honeymoon period—by and large resented by the Hindu majority, while the Muslim mystics attracted the low-caste Hindus and the Buddhist majority on the eastern and western rimlands of the subcontinent—the areas now constituting Bangladesh and Pakistan respectively. Hindu India, however, remained the Continent of Circe, assimilating the alien faith and culture as much as possible—so much so that a time came when a pre-Shankara Acharya period Hindu and his average educated counterpart during the reign of Akbar were barely comparable.

The Muslim-Hindu interaction demanded of the intelligentsia of both great religions the maximum spirit of tolerance and forbearance. In the process, both Hindu and Muslim societies enriched each other. Islam in India, though heavily indebted to central Asian influences and the Hanafi school of jurisprudence, did not come in the way of its native adherents' retaining some pre-Islamic influences which made it distinctively different from other Muslim societies in neighbouring Central Asia, Afghanistan, Iran, and other Middle Eastern societies.

Culture thus came to be regarded as something not co-extensive with religion. It is in rituals—from a child's birth to the last ritual of consigning the body of a dead person to the dust (from dust it sprang and to dust it went forth)—that much of real India continued to manifest itself, irrespective of the exterior of religious formalism. India on the eve of partition retained much of the common heritage evolved and developed over the centuries. The sharp turn in its political destiny notwithstanding, millions of families divided by the new borders could not change the many common living styles, languages, and cultural features whose effective similarities still bewilder a European, American, or African ethnologist and linguist. Pakistan's Muslim and India's Hindu populations cannot shut their eyes to the legacies of the Muslim and Hindu past lying on the other side of the border.

The book in your hands comprises articles by eight more or less well-known individuals, each prominent in their own field. Each writer sets out to explore, on the fiftieth anniversary of Freedom, the common heritage of the subcontinent on the eve of partition. Each provides a vivid picture of the segment of life to which he or she was witness, leading the reader to wonder what it was that made the transfer of power to a united India impossible. Was it a historical process—silent and invisible, working its way towards the inevitable turn of destiny—or was it the force of circumstances, as is commonly believed?

The contributors to this volume from India are Aruna Asaf Ali, B. K. Nehru, Khushwant Singh, and Pandu Chintamani. Khushwant Singh talks about his Lahore memories, although the rest do not have memories of

Pakistan to dwell upon. Their focus is Indian life and the common heritage it signified.

The participants from Pakistan are Shaista Ikramullah, Mukhtar Zaman, Shehla Shibli, and Akhtar Payami. Each one has touched upon the common heritage. Shaista Ikramullah was one of the first Muslim women to be elected to the first Constituent Assembly of Pakistan. Her husband was one of the first Muslims to be an ICS officer, and rose to be Pakistan's first Foreign Secretary. Shehla Shibli a well-known journalist who comes from a prominent Hindu family of Kashmir, married a Muslim, and is well-connected to the Muslim, Hindu, and Sikh aristocracy of the Punjab. Mukhtar Zaman has the distinction of being the President of the Muslim Students Federation, an arm of the Muslim League during the Freedom struggle, and Akhtar Payami is a prominent journalist. All of them belong to divided families.

Reading the Indian and Pakistani writers' accounts, one is led to wonder how it is that a society which was, barring a few obvious cases, exemplary in its communal adjustments and accommodation, made an about-turn in reaching the 'D-Day' target set by the last Viceroy, Lord Mountbatten. When he struck the Union Jack to the dying notes of 'God Save the King', what an anti-climax to the position of unbridled sway of British rule over a vast subcontinent, which had included Burma and Ceylon at some points of time.

Let us journey into the past—not a distant past. When the Muslims made their inroads into India they termed its denizens 'Hindus' only geographically, as al-Biruni did in his *Indica*. Edward Balfour's *Encyclopedia of India* (published 1858) contains the following statement: 'Hindu is entirely a European conventional term and does not represent a nation, a race or a religion...' Jawaharlal Nehru in his *Discovery of India* admits that the word 'Hindu' does not occur at all in our ancient literature. It was the geographical term 'Hindu', coined by the Muslims, which was finally adopted even by the British rulers to describe all native Indians other than the monotheist Muslims. Possibly the word was meant to identify the amalgam of Dravidian and Aryan faith which centred round Vedantic animism.

It was as a response to Muslim rule in Sindh that Shankara Acharya set about structuring Hindu society around the basis of a caste system. The emphasis on Brahma encompassing Shiva and Vishnu was also intended to contend with Islamic monotheism. The Bhakti movement, it is held by some scholars, was a response to the challenge of Islamic mysticism. In the process the Bhakti-Sufi legacy flourished. Aruna Asaf Ali's article articulates on this theme, and it requires a detailed study of the phenomenon to appreciate this development.

It was during the reign of Jehangir that Mujaddid Alif Sani (1563-1624) initiated a movement which sought to counter the increasing intermingling of Hindus and Muslims, matters having reached a point where it was not possible to distinguish one from the other.

The structure of Indian society during the Mughal period was based on class rather than on religion. The Mughals and Rajputs reached a consensus to share power. Intermarriage between the Mughal and Rajput aristocracies was common and there was much 'Indianization' or 'Hinduization' of Islam. A study of Nawab Dargah Quli Khan's social history of Delhi entitled *Muraqqa-i-Dehli* (Portrait of Delhi) proves this, whereas in Titu Mir's Bengal of the eighteenth century, Hindu revivalism had given rise to Muslim revivalism seeking a return to puritanical Islam. Shah Waliullah's efforts to encourage a similar revival did not impress upon the common masses or the aristocracy, whereas in Bengal, Titu Mir's movement did motivate the masses. In Delhi and around the imperial capital the revivalist movement attracted the attention of the educated Muslims whose lifestyle was threatened by the decay of Mughal power and the rise of the East India Company.

It is noteworthy that the challenge-response syndrome of Hindu-Muslim revivalism intensified with the rise of foreign power. With the decay of the Mughals the majority community of India thought that their best opportunity of consolidating themselves and regaining their lost glory lay with the foreigners.

The important Muslim revivalist movements led by Mujaddid Alif Sani, Shah Waliullah (1703-61) and Syed Ahmed Shaheed (1786-1831), exhorted the Muslims to return to pure Islam, leaving *en route* the encrustations of Hindu influence. Even Sir Syed's advocacy of Western education—mainly the teaching of English, Science, and Technology—could be considered as a movement to help Muslims regain their lost glory through modern education. Revivalists and modernists acted like a pincer movement, seeking to inculcate the idea of Muslims being a separate nation seeking its own social, economic, and political goals. The Hindu revivalists in Bengal, and efforts to curb the Muslim peasantry through crippling taxes (even on growing beards and on constructing a mosque) in conjunction with the British, made the emergence of Titu Mir and Haji Shariatullah possible.

In the North the Mujahideen Movement flourished to arrest Muslim decay—the British government offered no resistance to it since it sought to fight the Sikhs, who had banned certain *Shaair* (rituals) of Islam such as *Azan,* and had made predatory raids on the Muslim chieftains of Multan and Bahawalpur.

The 1920s saw Dr Moonje and Shradanand exhorting the Hindus to convert Muslims to Hinduism. This movement precipitated Muslim exclusivism still further. The last two decades of the nineteenth century and the first decade of the twentieth century caused incalculable damage to the foundations of the Common Legacy. It was not until the last half of the second decade of this century that the remarkable Hindu-Muslim unity was witnessed, and that too from the platform of the Khilafat Movement. It is interesting to note that the Rector of Deoband, Maulana Mahmood Hasan, headed the Raishmi Roomal Movement around 1913-14 which helped the formation of an Indian Government-in-exile in Kabul comprising Hindu and Muslim leaders. The Aligarh Movement, which sought to inculcate in Muslims loyalty to the British Raj, was sidelined, and the Congress leaders were seen moving in and out of mosques all over India urging their Muslim compatriots to unite under one banner against the British.

In the early 1920s, hopes of a Hindu-Muslim *rapprochement* were dashed to the ground by the sudden burst of the *Shuddi-Sangathan* Movement aimed at proselytizing Muslims. Was it an accidental development, or a premeditated move to harm Hindu-Muslim unity, which had seen many ups and downs before? By 1924-5 communal harmony had suffered incalculable damage. And the situation went on worsening, to the extent that the three successive Round Table Conferences and even the 1935 Act could not satisfy the aspirations of the major communities of India.

The years 1919-21 could be regarded as the honeymoon period of the marriage between politically active Muslims and Hindus. The Khilafat Movement had attracted Mahatma Gandhi, Malaviya, and Motilal Nehru's active and willing co-operation. There is no doubt that until then the majority of Muslim leaders had regarded their Hindu compatriots as the main beneficiaries of the demise of whatever was left of Muslim influence in the wake of the fiasco of the 'War of Independence' or 'Mutiny' of 1857. The Hindus had greatly benefited from the gradual transition of power from the Muslims to the British in the pre-1857 period, and the Muslims' grievances against the Hindus could be traced back to this very period—the period spanning Clive's empire-building and the implementation of Lord Macaulay's Minutes in 1835. Wilfred Cantwell Smith has aptly commented on this state of affairs:

The repression of the Muslims...keeping them out of the administration and of the medical, legal and other such professions, and in general not educating them, was, clearly, a policy affecting the upper and the potentially middle classes. It was at this time that the clerical and professional classes among the Hindus were developing and beginning to wield power. The India Office was afraid to allow the same power to the Muslims...More specially it was afraid to allow that power to both groups at the same time.

(*Modern Islam in India*, Lahore, 1947).

It is against this backdrop of Indian politics, which ensured mistrust and bickering between the two major communities of the subcontinent, that one can discern in the contributions of various eminent personalities from both sides of the borders, that lingering streak of communal harmony which survived the politics of mistrust that made the partition of the subcontinent inevitable.

One need not go into the details of the factors leading to 'the Great Divide', since it was amicably accepted by both the All-India Congress Committee and the All-India Muslim League as the only way out of the impasse created by the Congress President's refusal to accept Muhammad Ali Jinnah's conditions for the transfer of power to the united India on 10 July 1946 in a news conference at Bombay.

It is true that things were never the same again, and the communal drift kept on widening, so much so that the worst communal riots erupted in Bengal and Bihar, and the Punjab and Delhi were engulfed in a bloodbath, which makes B. K. Nehru, Aruna Asaf Ali, and Khushwant Singh's memories of communal harmony all the more poignant. B. K. Nehru's lament over the erosion of *mushtarika tahzeeb* (the common culture) is understandable. He is eminently right when he says:

The winds of change overtook the comfortable, leisurely, carefree, peaceful life that the upper class lived till only a few years before independence and partition. It had become increasingly clear over the years that no matter how much they might resent it, the British would some day or the other have to permit the Indians to take charge of their own destiny. Nobody in India was really aware that by the 1930s the will to power which was embodied in the doctrine of Imperialism had already disappeared in Britain. Nor could anybody foresee that Hitler would so weaken the colonial powers that after the War they would simply not have the strength to retain their unwilling colonies. The total disappearance of Britain from the Indian scene as early as 1947 was therefore unexpectedly premature.

Coming to Aruna Asaf Ali's contribution, 'The Bhakti-Sufi Legacy', one really wonders at how miserably the political pundits failed in assessing the fragility of the British Raj after the Second World War and the inevitability of partition when the people, avowedly anti-partition, were doing all they could to make it inevitable. An extract from Asaf Ali's diary for 14 October 1944 is worth noting:

> Blind sentiment rooted in history seems to have proved too strong for a confident and united bid for freedom. Perhaps not until Hindustan and Pakistan have actually worked as free countries for sometime will either Hindus or Muslims and others begin to see things in proper perspective. If so, well, let even a divided India begin to function as a co-operative commonwealth of sovereign states.

Even the pious wish expressed in the preceding paragraph appears to be a tall order. We read in Khushwant Singh's interesting construct of life in pre-partition Lahore the death of an illusion, and finally we see 'tears of joy blurring' his vision as he hears buglers sound the 'Last Post' as Lord Mountbatten lowers the Union Jack from the

Red Fort. History did not allow anyone to sustain and nurture illusions when the divisive die was finally cast.

Shaista Ikramullah's contribution, 'The Common Heritage', and Pandu Chintamani's sentimental recollection, 'The Hindu Son', corroborate each others' memories of what once looked to be the order of the day. Ultimately, though, the world they remember seems to be escaping us, like clouds in the sky on a typical post-monsoon day, when sun and cloud play a blissful game of hide-and-seek with each other.

The other accounts—by Shehla Shibli, Akhtar Payami, and Mukhtar Zaman—also endorse those by Nehru, Aruna Asaf Ali, and Khushwant Singh of memories strengthening the theme of a communal harmony that subsisted not only between the elite classes—overriding religious distinctions—but also the working classes and lower middle class.

The middle class, locked as it was in the battle to obtain as many employment opportunities as possible, has almost everywhere been more brittle and more short-term-goal oriented, and has always had a tendency to burst at the seams. The subcontinent was no exception, and neither are the present-day India and Pakistan. The middle class is a critical mass and much 'communal' heat has been generated by this class. And we know that a class which has to fight for its existence readily ignites.

So the story of the Common Heritage is a story worth telling. There are individuals living on both sides of the border who could tell similar stories of communal harmony in their respective countries. The Oxford University Press has done well to publish recollections of some important personalities in the year of the Golden Jubilee Celebrations of Pakistan and India. I believe that there ought to be a good number of outstanding personalities who owe it to posterity to share their memories so as to enable younger people to appreciate the riches of our common heritage and culture. I wonder why it could not be richer still when

Pakistan, India, and Bangladesh exist on the map of the world as three independent and sovereign countries taking pride in their common past. Our wish, however, ought to be that this selective band of experiences may expand its magnitude and that all of us may live as though we cherish humanistic values for the promotion of higher values of life.

Muhammad Ali Siddiqui
21 April 1997

Khushwant Singh

India's best-known columnist, and one of its most famous and widely read authors, Khushwant Singh is witty, articulate, sometimes shocking, and always entertaining.

He was born in 1915 in Hadali, Punjab, and educated at Government College Lahore, King's College, and the Inner Temple in London. After he left his law practice he joined the Indian Ministry of Foreign Affairs in 1947, and was sent on diplomatic postings to Canada and London, and later to Paris with UNESCO.

His journalistic career spans almost five decades, during which he was the editor of celebrated publications such as *Yojna* (1951-3), *Illustrated Weekly of India* (1969-79), *National Herald* (1978-9), and *Hindustan Times* (1980-3).

His first novel, *Train to Pakistan* won him the Grove Press Award for the best work of fiction in 1954; his other novels include *I Shall Not Hear the Nightingale* and *Delhi*. He has also published a two-volume history of the Sikhs, several translated works, and non-fiction works on Delhi, nature, and current affairs.

Khushwant Singh was a Member of Parliament (1980-6), and received numerous awards in recognition of his services. In 1984, he returned the Padma Bhushan, awarded him in 1974, in the wake of the Golden Temple tragedy.

Lahore, Partition, and Independence

Khushwant Singh

Having spent two carefree years in Government College, I was no stranger to Lahore. But coming there to earn my living was a different matter. I had everything laid on for me—a well-furnished flat and office, membership of the two leading clubs, the Cosmopolitan, meant for the Indian elite, and the more exclusive Gymkhana, which was largely an English preserve with no more than a dozen Oxbridge-educated 'natives'. My father's and father-in-law's status opened the doors of judges and ministers to me. With my young and attractive wife, we soon became the most sought-after and photographed couple in Lahore.

The only thing missing was the clientele. I spent a couple of hours in the morning in my office pouring over law books, then went to the Bar Room for gossip. I went to the Courtrooms to hear important cases being argued, spent an hour or so in the Coffee House for more gossip, and returned for lunch. For the first few months not a single litigant crossed my threshold. For a while I worked as a junior to Kirpa Narain, who had moved from Delhi to Lahore. One day he collapsed and died while arguing a case. I shifted over as junior to Jai Gopal Sethi, who had the largest criminal practice in the Punjab. He occasionally got his clients to throw a few crumbs as junior's fees at me. I was told that I should acquire a good *munshi*, or clerk. They are quite an institution in the Indian legal profession. Where there are no solicitors, as in the Punjab, they do the soliciting—talking to clients, sorting out their papers, fixing the fee to be extracted, extracting it along with their *munshiana* of ten per cent. Many did much more. They went to the railway stations and bus stands as hotel agents do, spotted litigants and persuaded them to take on their employer as their advocate. All manner of persuasion was practised: their master's wife was the judge's mistress, or vice versa, or he was the ablest 'England-returned Barrister', who played tennis and bridge with the *Sahibs*, drank and danced with their *mems*.

The first clerk I hired was a sharp little fellow from Himachal. He persuaded me to let him go on tour in Punjab's districts to do propaganda for me. He was away for a month, presented me his travel bills, and assured me that many leading lawyers of the district courts had promised to send their appellate work to me. None came.

The second one was a Shia Muslim. He got me a brief as a junior to a leading lawyer from Lucknow in a case involving two branches of rich Shia *zamindars* of Bahraich over their property in Lahore. I got a small fee but lost the friendship of the Lahore head of the family. We also lost the case. Thereafter having nothing to do, I let my *munshi* hire a *maulvi* who taught me the Koran for an hour every morning. Some time later the *munshi* left me on the pretext that taking a salary from a non-believer who was not only not a Muslim but who did not believe in God was *haraam*, unlawful.

In sheer desperation I hired the most expensive *munshi* in Lahore. He was a strapping, six-foot Sikh Jat who was a renowned tout. I paid him Rs 10,000 as advance—a sum unheard of—to secure his services.

He was familiar with Sikh villages in Lahore district. Whenever there was a murder in any village—and there were at least three or four every month—he went to condole with the bereaved family as well as call on the family whose members had been named as accused. He managed to get a brief from one side or the other. Instead of the tenth due to him as *munshiana*, he took a third of my fee.

However, criminal cases started coming my way. I won some, lost others. I also discovered that hiring renowned lawyers at high fees did not really make much difference in a criminal case. If a magistrate or judge was friendly towards me, I got bail for my clients. And often a lighter sentence. There was an Anglo-Indian lawyer who knew hardly any law but managed to get cases through his touts because he was a *sahib*. Also a Parsee who wore a monocle, hummed and hawed his way through his briefs in a fake upper-class English accent, and managed to make a reasonable living. There was a Muslim lawyer who gained notoriety for never preparing his briefs and throwing his clients on the mercy of the court. 'Who knows the law better than Your Honour? Who am I to tell you the real facts of the case? Your Honour will no doubt grasp them better than I and do justice to my client!' Believe it or not, he did better than most lawyers who burned the midnight oil pouring over their briefs and wrangled with judges.

It was a hard, back-breaking, soulless profession. I took on undefended cases in Sessions Courts for a fee of Rs 16 per day; I appeared free of charge in cases against communists; I took on part-time teaching at the Law College; I was put on the panel of defence lawyers at the High Court and then on the panel of the Advocate General. I hardly ever made more than a thousand rupees a month. My father continued to subsidize me. He bought me a larger apartment with property which brought me some rent; then a large house on Lawrence Road facing Lahore's biggest park, Lawrence Gardens, (later renamed Bagh-e-Jinnah). None of this made me change my opinion of the legal profession.

Perhaps it was my failure to make it in a big way that soured me. I kept asking myself, 'Is there anything creative in practising law? Don't I owe more to the one life I have than making money out of other peoples' quarrels? A common prostitute renders more service to society than a lawyer. If anything the comparison with the whore is unfair to her. She at least serves a social need, and gives her clients pleasure for their money; a lawyer doesn't even do that.' I have little doubt that if I had stuck to the law a little longer, I would have made it to the Bench and perhaps even to the Supreme Court. Jokers with less practice than me and lesser legal acumen were elevated to the Bench; a couple ended up as Judges of the Supreme Court. Never did I regret chucking up the law; my only regret was that I wasted five years studying it and another seven trying to make a living out of it.

* * *

Having not much to keep me in the law courts, I began to read books which I should have read in my years in college: anthologies of English poetry, Shakespeare's plays and sonnets, Tolstoy, Oscar Wilde, Aldous Huxley, Hindu philosophy by Radhakrishnan. I also began to review books for *The Tribune* and wrote a short eulogistic booklet on Stalin for the Friends of the Soviet Union, of which I was a founder member. When on vacation in Mashobra I did little besides reading in the mornings and taking long walks in the afternoons. Every afternoon I strode alongside my wife, who was on a bicycle, six miles down to Simla. We had tea at Wenger's or Davico's, watched the pageant of English officials, Indian Ministers, and their over-dressed wives strolling along the Mall. And then six miles back to Mashobra. Once Sir Charles Carson, Finance Minister of the Maharaja of Gwalior, spent a couple of days with us. He told me that he had walked to Tatapani hot springs, on the banks of the Sutlej 5000 feet below Simla, and back, in a day. The following weekend I did the same. I bathed in the sulphur spring, drank a bottle of beer cooled in the icy, fast-running Sutlej, and was back home in time for dinner. Once I took a bet with my sister's husband, Jaspal Singh, who was as tough a Sikh Jat as I had met, that I could outwalk him. We set out on a full-moon-lit night on the

Hindustan-Tibet road. He had two of his nephews with him, both in their early twenties, and two Kashmiri porters to carry our provisions. After fifteen miles, the two boys and the porters refused to go any further. We left them at a *dak* bungalow and proceeded towards our destination, Narkanda. Later that night we stopped at another *dak* bungalow in the midst of a fir forest to refresh ourselves. Jaspal drank milk by the gallon; I took hot tea laced with brandy. It was eerie in the moonlit stillness. We were talking very loudly when out of the seemingly untenanted bungalow came a loud yell, 'b...off!' We did. We arrived at Narkanda early in the morning. We took whatever the chowkidar could give us: *ghee parathas* and over-sweetened tea. We started our journey back home. We kept pace all day and late into the evening. My feet began to bleed. At a *dak* bungalow about ten miles from Mashobra I stopped to tie them with rags provided by the *chowkidar*. Jaspal decided to go ahead to claim victory. I followed a hundred yards behind him. He got to Mashobra at about midnight, told the family that I had given up on the way, and went triumphantly to bed. I went straight to my bedroom. He was boasting about his feat at the breakfast table when I joined him. Technically he had won. We had done seventy-two miles more or less non-stop. Both of us spent the next few days nursing our sore feet. 'If you had worked for seventy-two hours instead of walking seventy-two miles, you would have been a wiser man,' was the only comment my father made. I was not allowed to undertake any more long walks. But a fortnight later, when my father was away in Delhi, I had to return to Lahore on some business. I decided to walk down to Kalka, which was sixty-five miles away, downhill most of the way. I left Mashobra while it was still dark. I got to Dharampur (fifty miles) by the afternoon and was having tea at the rest house when suddenly my father turned up and joined me for tea. It occurred to him that I did not have a taxi waiting for me. 'Where is your taxi?' he asked me. I had to admit I had walked down all the way. He lost his temper and ordered his chauffeur to get a taxi to Kalka and saw me ride away in it. A Great pity! The one thing I looked forward to after the marathon walk to Kalka was a shower at the railway station followed by a bottle of chilled beer and a sumptuous meal.

* * *

I have the happiest of memories of the summer months I spent in my parents' beautiful house in Mashobra. It occupied an entire hill, giving a spectacular view of snow-clad mountains to the north and deep valleys on the other side. My mother had a large cement platform raised which overlooked the road running from Simla to Mashobra bazaar, Gables Hotel, past the estate of the Raja of Faridkot, to a nine-hole golf course at Naldera. We spent most of our mornings and afternoons on this platform, sunning ourselves, or in the shade of a holly-oak which stood alongside it. The bird-life was fantastic. Barbets cried all day long. Flocks of scarlet minivets flew among the cherry trees. Sibias nested in a creeper-covered elm. Flycatchers, including the spectacular silver-white paradise flycatcher with his two ribbons of tail trailing behind him, were not an uncommon sight. Lammergeiers and Himalayan eagles floated in the air. Early mornings and late evenings blackbirds perched on our roof and broke into song. All through moonlit nights, night-jars called to each other. A family of flying squirrels had their nest in our eaves; we often saw them float down from tree to tree and hop about on the tennis court.

Sundays were special. We woke to the peal of bells from St Swithin's Church at the entrance to Mashobra Bazaar. It had been built by Allen, a leather-merchant of Kanpur, and was named after the patron saint of cobblers. It was exactly like a village chapel in England, with a lych-gate, stained glass windows, and High Altar. English folk staying at Gables and Wild Flower Hall on the crest of the hill

trooped in in their Sunday best for the morning service.
Thereafter they strolled about the bazaar exuding the
fragrance of lavender and French perfumes.

My father was an Anglophile and loved entertaining.
Once he sent invitations to all the European residents of
Wild Flower Hall and Gables. They came in their dozens
because it was wartime and nothing very exciting happened
in Simla. We hung Chinese lanterns all the way from the
entrance gate up to our house. We had a Goan band to
play dance music. The *Sahibs* introduced themselves and
their *mems*, drank our Scotch and wines, ate our curried
meal, danced, and departed. The next morning I asked my
father if it had been worthwhile blowing up thousands of
rupees entertaining total strangers. 'English people never
forget anyone who is hospitable to them,' he replied. He
was right. A few days later, when he was going down to
Delhi, an English officer came to him in the rail-car and
introduced himself as one who had been at his party. They
got talking. My father landed a very lucrative contract to
supply provisions to the army.

The Raja of Faridkot was also very fond of entertaining
white people. Every autumn he would arrange bull-fights
in an open arena. Villagers came in their thousands
bringing their champion bulls. Foreign and important
Indian guests sat on sofas watching the bulls tangle with
each other. After the show, the Raja entertained his guests
at a banquet with his private band playing. Since we often
had English friends staying with us, we were often invited.
The Raja could be as generous as he could be mean. He
served champagne to everyone, but when it came to whisky,
his bearers served Indian whisky to Indians, Scotch only to
the whites. I discovered this one evening when we took
Evan Charlton, editor of *The Statesman,* and his wife Joy
with us to one of his parties. When I complained to Evan
about the quality of the whisky he snorted, 'You are a
suspicious so-and-so! My whisky is okay.' We exchanged
glasses. He wrinkled his nose when he tasted mine. The

Raja could also be very uncouth. Whenever my father invited him, he would drink himself silly and stay on after all the other guests had left. He made passes at my nieces, then only in their teens, and at other young women around. My poor parents, who usually retired at 9 p.m., were kept up till midnight.

More than anything else I loved my long evening walks. When not bound for Simla, I explored other mountain roads. There was a solitary, shaded path which ran through a pine and fir forest to an Italian monastery called San Demiano. Another went steeply uphill from Mashobra to a small orchard called Danes Folly towards Wild Flower Hotel. From the top of the hill you could see the mountain range with Shali peak rising to above 10,000 feet and a broad stream dividing the two ranges. During the rainy season, the Valley was often covered over by mists. Mysteriously the mists would lift and the sun break through, lighting the rain-washed, emerald green hillsides and setting the stream that ran between them sparkling in the sunlight.

Once a year in the autumn there was a fair in village Sipi, a mile or so below Mashobra bazaar. Villagers brought their nubile daughters and young sons to arrange marriages for them. It was rumoured that pretty girls—Himachal girls can be fair, petite, almond-eyed and wanton—were put up for sale to the highest bidder. I saw many pretty village lasses but never saw one being taken away by any outsider.

* * *

Not having much to do in Lahore and yet possessing a nice home and a lovely-looking (though by now somewhat over-assertive) wife, I had no dearth of visitors. Foremost among these was my friend Mangat Rai, who was posted there. Being in the ICS he was much sought after by Christian fathers with marriageable daughters. He also wrote pieces which he read out to an ever-admiring circle of friends. One which received encores was about a hen which laid eggs in a drain. It was always heard with open-mouthed admiration. He became a daily visitor to my apartment. Every evening after his office he hauled his bicycle up the stairs and often stayed on for drinks and dinner. Whatever reservations he had about my wife vanished; it was evident that he was getting quite enamoured of her. To leave me in no doubt he wrote me a letter confessing that he was in love with her and seeking my permission to continue visiting us. I passed this letter on to my wife. I could see that she was highly flattered. I treated it as a joke and wrote back assuring him that he would be as welcome as before. I had reason to regret my magnanimity. Mangat Rai had enormously persuasive powers to bring people round to his point of view. Most of it was destructive and designed to reduce others to plasticine that he could mould in whatever shape he wanted. My wife at the time spent some hours every morning at a painting studio run by Bhubesh Sanyal. He began dropping in at the studio and persuaded her that painting was a futile pastime. She gave up painting. She was a very keen tennis player and always spent the evenings playing with me at the club. He persuaded her that cycling was more fun, so she abandoned tennis and went cycling with him. She was very punctilious about religious ritual: opening the *Granth Sahib* every morning, reading a hymn or two, and wrapping it up in the evening. He convinced her of the futility of ritual. She began to miss out on her daily routine of prayers and ritual. He had become a hard drinker. My wife took to drinking hard. He was very open about everything he did. He told my wife that one evening, when seeing off his sister at the railway station, he had run into a young Christian girl known to us. She had no transportation. He offered to ride her back on his cycle. She sat on the front bar. He invited her to his apartment without any conditions attached. She accepted. They spent the night in the same bed. He admitted he felt a little guilty because he loved her and not the girl he had bedded. Instead of feeling let down, my wife admired his candour and was more drawn to him. Inevitably their association came to be much talked about.

Amongst others who became regular visitors to my home were Justice Gopal Das Khosla, also of the ICS, and his wife Shakuntala. He was taken with my wife; I with his. So we were on the level. Then there was the Canadian couple, Wilfred Cantwell-Smith, Scholar of Islamics working on Indian Islam, and his wife Muriel, working for a doctor's degree at the Medical College. There was P.N. Kirpal, then lecturer of history at Dayal Singh College. He was destined to stay in our lives for the rest of our days. There were others like Nawabzada Mahmood Ali Khan and his Sikh wife Satnam; Wilburn and Usha Lal who were distantly related to Mangat Rai; Professor Inder Mohan Varma, lecturer in English at the Government College; Bishen Narain and his wife Shanti, both friends of the Khoslas. Others came and went. Occasionally, when he was in Lahore, there was Arthur's younger brother John Lall, also in the ICS. John was a bit of a playboy with an incredibly British accent. He was given to making wisecracks at my expense. 'Kaval,' he said to my wife one day, 'if you have a sister let her marry your bearded husband and you marry me.' I was the target of witticisms from both the Lall brothers. With John I settled scores when he brought his fiancée Hope, a dark, pudgy girl, to introduce to us. The next day he dropped in he asked me what I thought of her. 'She will be a perpetual exercise in faith and charity,' I told him. He made no wisecracks thereafter. My day of reckoning with Arthur had to wait some years.

Two people who I met in my early years in Lahore deserve mention. One was the painter, Amrita Sher Gill. Her fame had preceded her before she took up residence in a block of flats across the road from ours. She had recently married her Hungarian cousin, Victor Egan, a doctor of medicine who wanted to set up practice in Lahore. Amrita was said to be very beautiful and very promiscuous. Pandit Nehru was known to have succumbed to her charms; stories of her sexual appetite were narrated with a lot of slavering.

I didn't know how much truth there was to gossip of her being a nymphomaniac, but I was eager to get to know her. I did not have to wait for very long. It was summertime. My wife and six-month-old son had gone up to Kasauli to stay with her parents. One afternoon when I came home for lunch I found a tankard of beer and a lady's handbag on a table in my sitting room and a heavy aroma of French perfume. I tiptoed to the kitchen to ask my cook who it was. 'I don't know,' he replied, 'a *memsahib* in a sari. She asked for you. I told her you would soon be back for lunch. She looked round the flat and helped herself to the beer from the fridge. She is in the bathroom.' I knew it could only be Amrita Sher Gill. And so it was. She came into the sitting room and introduced herself. She told me of the flat she had rented across the road and wanted advice about carpenters, plumbers, tailors, and the like. I told her whatever I knew about such people. I tried to size her up. I couldn't look her in the face because she had that bold, brazen kind of look which made a timid man like me turn his gaze downwards. She was short in stature and sallow complexioned (being half Sikh, half Hungarian). Her hair was parted in the middle and severely bound at the back. She had a bulbous nose with blackheads showing. She was full-lipped with faint traces of a moustache on her upper lip. I told her I had heard a lot about her paintings and pointed to some water colours on the wall which my wife had done. 'She is just learning to paint,' I said by way of explanation. 'That's obvious,' she snorted. Politeness was not one of her virtues; she believed in speaking her mind however rude or unkind it might be.

A few weeks later I had another sample of her rudeness. I had picked up my wife and son from Kasauli and taken them up to Mashobra. Amrita was staying with her friends the Chaman Lals, who had rented a house a little above my father's. I invited them for lunch. We were having beer and gin slings on the open platform under the shade of the holly-oak. My son was in a playpen learning to stand on his own feet. Everyone was paying him compliments: he was indeed a very pretty little child with curly hair, large eyes, and dimpled cheeks. 'What an ugly little boy!' remarked Amrita. Others protested their embarrassment. My wife froze. Amrita continued to drink her beer without concern. Later, when she heard what my wife had to say about her manners, and that she had described her as a bloody bitch, Amrita told her informant, 'I'll teach that woman a lesson. I'll seduce her husband.'

I waited eagerly for the day of seduction. It never came. When we returned to Lahore, my wife declared our home out of bounds for Amrita. Some common friends told us that Amrita was not keeping well. One night a cousin of hers came over to spend the night with us because Amrita was too ill to have guests. He told us that she was in a delirium and kept mumbling calls at bridge—she was an avid bridge player. Next morning we heard she was dead. She was only thirty-one.

I went over to her apartment. Her old, bearded father Umrao Singh was in a daze, her mother in a state of hysterics. They had just arrived from Summer Hill (Simla) and could not believe that their young, talented daughter was gone for ever.

That afternoon a dozen of us followed her cortege to the cremation ground where her husband set alight her funeral pyre. When we returned to the Egans' apartment, the police were waiting for him. England had declared war on Hungary as an ally of Nazi Germany. Egan was an enemy national. He was lucky to have been taken into police custody.

It took some time for Amrita's mother to get the details of her daughter's illness and death. She held her nephew and son-in-law responsible for it. She bombarded ministers, officials, friends (including myself) with letters accusing him of murder. Murder, I am certain it was not.

Carelessness, I am equally certain, it was. My version of her death came from Dr Raghubir Singh, then a leading physician of Lahore. He was summoned to her bedside at midnight when she was beyond hope of recovery. He believed that she had become pregnant and had been aborted by her husband. The operation had gone wrong. She had bled profusely and developed peritonitis. Her husband wanted Dr Raghubir Singh to give her a blood transfusion and offered his own blood for it. Dr Raghubir Singh refused to do so without finding out their blood grouping. While the two doctors were arguing with each other, Amrita slipped out of life.

Many people, such as the art critic Karl Khandalawala, Iqbal Singh, and her nephew, the painter Vivan Sundaram, have written about Amrita. Badruddin Tyabji has given a vivid account of how he was seduced by her. Vivan admits she had many lovers. Her real passion in life was another woman—she was also lesbian. And she was a superb painter.

* * *

Among the guests who stayed in my apartment while my wife and son were away for the summer was the Communist Danial Latifi. He had been in and out of jail and the food they gave him at the Party headquarters did not agree with him. Being at the time close to the Party, I invited him to spend some weeks with me to recoup his health. Danial was then, as he is today, a compulsive talker. His flat, monotone voice retains the same soporific quality. One evening two of my friends dropped in. Both were very drunk. Danial converted their polite queries into a long monologue on dialectical materialism and the class struggle. I went out to take some fresh air. When I returned half an hour later, Danial was still holding forth. Both my friends were fast asleep. Through Danial I received two other visitors in turn. The first was Sripad Dange, then on the run from the police. He had to pretend to be my servant. He spent most of his time reading my books. When anyone came to see me he would disappear into the kitchen. Another was Ajoy Ghosh, also then underground. He was a dour, uncommunicative man. His mistress and later wife, Litto, dropped in every day and spent many hours with him when I was at the High Court. Many years later, in England, I asked my friend Everette of the CID if he had known of these men having stayed with me. He said he had, but it had been decided not to arrest them, only to keep a watch on my apartment and note down the names of people who came to visit them.

* * *

A person who dominated my life in my Lahore years was Manzur Qadir. He was a couple of years older than me, had done his Bar in England, and had practised in the district courts at Lyallpur. He had picked up a considerable practice and a reputation as an upright man of uncommon ability. His father, Sir Abdul Qadir, had been a judge of the Lahore High Court and a literateur: as editor of *Makhzan* he was the first to publish poems of Allama Iqbal. Manzur had married Asghari, the daughter of Mian Sir Fazal Hussain. She had been married earlier to the profligate Nawab of Hoti Mardan and had a daughter by him. The daughter had died and she had divorced her husband. She was a great beauty—the Russian artist Svetoslav Roerich had used her as a model for his paintings of the Madonna. At the time Asghari considered Manzur below her 'imperial' status and felt she had done him a great favour. He was a short, balding, beady-eyed man wearing thick glasses. He was evidently very much in love with his wife and patiently suffered her tantrums. They moved to Lahore with their daughter Shireen, who was the same age as my son Rahul. In Lahore they had a son, Basharat, who was two years younger than Shireen. It did not take long for Manzur and I to get acquainted and become friends. Fortunately our respective wives, both equally prickly characters, also hit it off well. We began to eat in each other's homes every day. My wife shared Manzur's enthusiasm for the cinema: they saw at least one picture together every week; also his passion for mangoes. Between them they would demolish a dozen at one sitting with great gusto.

Manzur was by any standards a most unusual character. He was without doubt the ablest up-and-coming lawyer in the Punjab. He and his uncle, Mohammad Saleem, the famous tennis player who represented India in the Davis Cup for fifteen years, spent hours arguing points of law after they had done a day's work in the High Court. Both men observed the highest standards of rectitude. They took their fees by cheque, or, when paid in cash, gave receipts for the full amount to their clients. They often paid more income tax than was due from them and had some of it refunded. Manzur was the only person I met in my life who never told a lie and took great pains to avoid hurting people's feelings. In due course, he became a kind of litmus paper by which his friends tested their own integrity. When in doubt over a course of action, we could ask ourselves, 'Will Manzur approve of this?' Like me he was an agnostic.

What Manzur and I also shared in common was a love for literature. In his case it was entirely Urdu poetry, to which he re-opened my eyes. He knew the works of many poets and could recite by the hour. He also tried his hand at writing, but without much success. He was best at composing bawdy verse which he recited with great verve to his circle of male friends, although he was extremely proper when women were around.

We spent many vacations together, sometimes at Patiala, where my father-in-law Sir Teja Singh Malik was a minister; other times in Delhi or Mashobra with my parents. Our friendship became the talk of the town as instances of such close friendships between Sikhs and Muslims or between Hindus and Muslims were very rare.

What proved to be a turning point in my career was Mangat Rai's desire to score over others of our circle as a man of letters. He suggested that, instead of him alone reading his pieces to an admiring audience, everyone should read something he or she had written. Our first meeting was in his home, a portion he had rented on Warris Road. The theme suggested by him was 'I believe'. We were to write down our beliefs on the values of life. About ten short papers were read out. I put down my reasons for disbelief in God and religion, and talked about friendship, love, marriage, death, and theories of life thereafter. There was nothing very original in what I wrote but just as it came to me. My main achievement was that I emerged as a rival to the hitherto unrivalled Mangat Rai. To be fair to him, he was generous in his praise. The next day I received a note of appreciation from Wilfred and Muriel Smith. It was my first fan mail and did a lot to boost my morale. Perhaps there was a little more to me than I thought.

The literary circle became a weekly feature. We met in different homes by rotation. A lot of liquor (mostly Indian brew) was consumed as poems, short stories, and essays were read and faithfully applauded by everyone. The two who contributed most were Justice G. D. Khosla and myself. Khosla was more anxious to establish himself as a writer than as a jurist. I had much less to do than any of the others. I used my visits to Sikh villages, from where my clients came, as background for my earlier stories. Mangat Rai's contributions as well as his attendance at our meetings began to dwindle. There were other reasons besides work for his absence.

Having come to the conclusion that he had little chance of wrecking my marriage as long as my wife's parents were alive, he began to cast around for a wife. The first to attract him was a very pretty girl, Lajwanti Rallia Ram, who belonged to a Nationalist Christian family. She was as fair as a Kashmiri Brahmin, large-eyed, tall, and slender. She got the top position in her MA English exam (her father happened to be Registrar of the University). I don't recall how they met, but since Mangat Rai was the most sought-after bachelor in the Christian community, the Rallia Rams could not have had much trouble discovering him and getting their daughter to meet him. The two often met in my apartment when we were away at the club. They announced their engagement and the wedding day was fixed. Wedding cards were printed and sent out. Lajwanti had her household linen embossed with the initials LMR. A few days before the marriage was to take place in a local church, Mangat Rai called it off. Lajwanti was heartbroken. Almost on the rebound she married Mohammed Yunus, a handsome Pathan who was active in the freedom movement. The marriage proved to be disastrous for both.

I could not make out why Mangat Rai had behaved the way he did towards Lajwanti. He had earlier got engaged to Indira Sarkar, younger sister of Professor K. M. Sarkar, and ditched her just as peremptorily when he got into the ICS. As soon as he was free of the second entanglement he resumed paying court to my wife and coming over to see us almost every day. I did not resent his visits as my wife had become extremely possessive, jealous, and demanding of attention. Her pre-occupation with Mangat Rai gave me relief.

A year or so later, Mangat Rai met another young Christian girl, Champa. She had also topped in the MA English exam when her father S. P. Singha was Registrar of the University. He was then in politics and had been elected to the Punjab Assembly from a Christian constituency. Champa was a very different kind of girl from Lajwanti. She was dusky, animated, and unihibited. She was known to have had quite a few affairs. Mangat Rai was drawn to her because of her vivacity. Champa and her parents knew that our opinion mattered a great deal to Mangat Rai and paid us a courtesy call. I did not tell them that I did not think their daughter and Mangat Rai would make a good marriage; she was too hot-blooded for him. However, they got engaged. Champa took no chances with a prolonged engagement and the two were married in church. Though invited, we did not attend the wedding. Champa made a few half-hearted attempts to befriend us. We did not respond. She decided to drop us.

As I had foreseen, the marriage proved to be a *mesalliance*. Mangat Rai resumed calling on us, and when we were away, writing to my wife regularly. However, his marriage went on the rocks in a more bizarre way than I had expected. One summer we were all together in Simla. The Mangat Rais were staying with his sister Sheila and her husband Arthur Lall in a house near the Lakkar Bazaar. We were, as usual, in my father's house in Mashobra. We cycled down to Simla every afternoon and spent the evenings strolling up and down the Mall with them. It was evident that Champa and Arthur were hitting it off very well. Arthur was not getting much out of his rather frigid wife and Mangat Rai was proving somewhat inadequate for Champa. Plans were made for a week's trekking into the interior. A party was formed and porters hired. On the last day Mangat Rai backed out. So did his sister Sheila. Arthur and Champa had a week together in the Himalayan fastness, spending their nights in deserted *dak* bungalows. They made up for what they had missed in their marriages. They returned from the trek convinced that they were made for each other. Mangat Rai readily agreed to divorce his wife; Sheila, a little reluctantly, conceded Arthur's wish to be free of her. It did not quite turn out that way. When the Singhas heard of it, they came down with a heavy hand on their daughter. Champa asked her husband to forgive her. He did so as readily as he had agreed to divorce her. But for all practical purposes the marriage was over. So was the Lalls'. After having bullied his wife into helping Champa get her passport (he had been given a posting in London) Arthur begged Sheila to return to him; he threatened to commit suicide if she did not forgive and forget. The high drama was to continue in the lives of all four of them. I was at times a spectator, at others a part of the cast.

* * *

My Lahore days were coming to an end. Almost from the day I had come to live there, war had been raging in Europe and the Far East. I had strong anti-fascist views and was convinced that Hitler, Mussolini, their European allies, and the Japanese had to be defeated before India could become free. Most Indians exulted in the victories of the Axis powers more out of spite for their English rulers than love for Nazis and Fascists. I wasn't quite sure of Japanese intentions after Subhas Chandra Bose took over command of the Indian National Army. He was too strong a man to be a puppet in anyone's hands. But even about him and his INA I had my doubts. My communist illusions were blown sky-high when Stalin made his pact with Hitler, and only partly restored when they went to war against each other. I did not approve of Gandhi's 'Quit India' Movement. I supported the Muslim demand for a separate state in areas where they were in a majority, believing that India would continue to remain one country with two autonomous Muslim-majority states at either end. I did not share any of the Hindu-Sikh suspicions or animosity against Muslims.

Not many Indians believed that the British would willingly relinquish their Empire in India. They regarded the Cripps and Cabinet Missions as eye-wash. They did not know the English. Young British officers who did their war service in India were a new breed. They refused to join exclusively white clubs, went out of their way to befriend Indians, expressed regret over what some English rulers had done in India, and sympathized with the Congress-led freedom movement. One event which re-assured me that independence was round the corner took place in the summer of 1946. I happened to be with my parents in

Mashobra. I had to return to Lahore, so I took the evening railcar to Kalka. There was only one other Indian besides me in the car, the rest were British officers in uniform and English civilians. After a brief halt at Barog for dinner we proceeded on our downhill journey. It was a beautiful full-moon night. At a bend near Dharampur, a wheel of the car came off the rails. The driver told us to wait till he got to the next station to order a relief car to be sent up from Kalka. We sat among the pines on a hillside bathed in moonlight. The English were understandably nervous as some months earlier a railcar had been ambushed by two robbers who had shot six English passengers and then run away without taking anything. It was suspected to be the handiwork of Indian terrorists. Somebody switched on the radio of the derailed car and tuned in to the BBC Overseas Service. Election results were being announced. The Labour Party had won a landslide victory and Clement Attlee was named Prime Minister of England. The English passengers heard the news in grave silence. The other Indian, whom I did not know, and I leapt up and embraced each other. We knew that with the Socialists in power in England, independence for India was indeed round the corner.

I had no illusions about the Muslim-Hindu/Sikh social divide. Even in the High Court Bar Association and Library, Muslim lawyers occupied different corners of the lounge and the library from Hindus and Sikhs. There was a certain amount of superficial mixing at weddings and funerals, but this was only to keep up appearances. After the Muslim League resolution demanding Pakistan, the cleavage became wide and continued to grow wider. The demand for Pakistan assumed the proportions of an avalanche gathering force as it went along. Every other afternoon huge processions of Muslims marched down the Mall chanting in unison:

Pakistan ka naaraah kya?
La illlaha illallah

What is the slogan of Pakistan?
There is but one God, He is Allah.

An instance of how deep the poison had spread was a case in which I appeared as Manzur's junior. It concerned a Sikh widow of considerable wealth and beauty named Sardarni Prem Prakash Kaur. She had been married to the only son of a wealthy contractor of Ludhiana. Her husband was a debauchee. He contracted syphilis and died without consummating his marriage. The entire estate came to the young widow. One day, while holidaying in Simla, she happened to be having tea at Davico's. A young Muslim strolling down the Mall saw her sitting alone by the window. Their eyes met and her smile assured him that he would not be unwelcome. He joined her for tea. They became lovers. The young man was handsome, but the good-for-nothing son of a barber. He began to live off Prem Prakash Kaur. They had two sons. Then Prem Prakash Kaur tired of her uncouth lover. Her cousin Gurnam Singh, as handsome as he was cultured, a Barrister-at-law with a large practice in Lyallpur (he was a close friend of Manzur Qadir) decided to rescue Prem Prakash from the clutches of the barber's son. Prem Prakash moved in with Gurnam. Her Muslim lover took her to court over the custody of the two boys. He claimed she had converted to Islam, married him by Islamic rites, and their boys were circumcised and given Muslim names. Besides marriage and custody of children, there were criminal cases of trespass and forcible seizure of property. As these cases moved from the lower courts to the appellate, the pattern became evident; if the presiding officer was Muslim, it went in favour of the barber's son; if Hindu or Sikh, in favour of the Sikh widow. I came in on the scene when the case of marriage and custody came up for hearing before Donald Falshaw, then a District and

Sessions Judge. I was engaged in order to give the case a non-communal flavour, as I was known to be friendly with Donald and his wife Joan.

But for the partition of India in August 1947, the case might still be going on. Prem Prakash Kaur and all her property were in East Punjab, which came to India. The barber's son was left in Pakistan. Gurnam migrated to East Punjab, became its Chief Minister, and resumed his liaison with Prem Prakash. He was later appointed Indian High Commissioner to Australia. A few days thereafter, returning home to collect his belongings, he was killed in an air crash.

* * *

The atmosphere became so charged with hate that it needed only a spark to set the Punjab ablaze. The year-long Hindu-Muslim riots in Calcutta led to massacres of Muslims in Bihar, then to massacres of Hindus in Noakhali in East Bengal. Then Muslims of the NWFP raided and scattered Sikh and Hindu villagers and slew as many as they could lay their hands on. Others fled their homes to safety in Lahore, Amritsar, and East Punjab.

While the killings of Hindus and Sikhs were going on in the NWFP, I happened to go to Abbottabad to appear as defence counsel in a murder case involving two branches of a Hindu family. The case was finished in one day. The next morning, instead of driving down to Taxila to catch my train, I decided to walk the distance of about eight to ten miles. It was balmy weather. I found the road absolutely deserted. Even villages through which I passed showed no signs of life. Men and women peeped out of their doorways to see me stride along. It was eerie. A couple of miles short of Taxila a lorry-load of Sikh soldiers pulled up beside me. A young Captain spoke harshly to me, 'Sardarji, are you out of your senses? They've killed every Sikh in these villages and you are out as if on an evening stroll. Get in.'

I obeyed and was dropped off at Taxila station. The railway station was also deserted except for the Station Master and a couple of ticket collectors. I saw the train I was to board come along and stop at the outer signal, I heard some shouting but could not make out what it was about. When the train pulled up on the platform, I got into a first class compartment. I was the only passenger. I bolted the door from the inside. There was no sign of life at any of the stations we passed through. When I got off the train at Lahore, the platform was deserted. There was not a porter in sight. Manzur Qadir had come to fetch me. He told me that communal riots had broken out in Lahore. The next morning I learnt from the papers that a train, the one on which I had travelled, had been held up at a signal near Taxila and all Sikh passengers had been dragged out and murdered.

A few days later, it was my turn to pick up Manzur Qadir. He had gone to do a case at Gujranwala. On his way back, when his train stopped at Badami Bagh, it was attacked by a Muslim mob and its Sikh passengers hauled out and hacked to death. He had seen the massacre with his own eyes. He looked bloodless and was still unsteady on his legs.

The last time I left Lahore before being forced to quit was to defend three men charged with robbery and murder in the court of the Sessions Judge at Gujranwala. Two of the accused had been members of the INA; I was engaged by an organization set up to defend them. This was not a political crime but a case of homicide. The men had boarded the night train from Lahore to Rawalpindi and forced their way into a first-class coupe occupied by two young English Army nurses. The girls put up resistance; one of them bit the man who tried to pull her down from the upper berth. The other fought back with her hands. The men threw her out of the fast-moving train. When the train stopped at Gujranwala, the three robbers disappeared in the darkness. The surviving girl ran up the platform screaming hysterically. Railway police came on the scene. They found the body of the other English girl lying along the track. The survivor was taken to Gujranwala hospital and treated for shock. The three accused were arrested the next day. They were Sikhs. They had woken up a barber at night and had him cut off their long hair and beards to escape detection. The surviving English girl was flown to England for treatment and was brought back after some months when the prosecution was ready to present its case. It felt it had a water-tight case based on the testimony of the barber and the recovery of stolen goods including a handbag with a compact, lipstick, comb, and other items of a lady's make-up from the accused. When I arrived in the Sessions Court it was clear that the Sessions Judge, a Muslim, had made up his mind to hang the three men. I pinned my hopes on the honesty of the English girl. I did not bother to cross-examine the barber at any length, nor the police over the recoveries made from the accused; village barbers could be made to say whatever the police wanted them to say; and planting incriminating articles on innocent people was a common practice. I concentrated entirely on the English girl. She was still in a state of shock and broke down many times while narrating the incidents of the fateful train journey. As I stood up to cross-examine her, the judge said to me very firmly: 'Be brief! She has been through a lot. I will not allow you to harass her.'

I protested equally firmly that I had to do my duty, or be allowed to withdraw from the case. He relented and allowed me to proceed. I asked the girl whether she could tell the difference between one Sikh and another if they happened to be of roughly the same age. She admitted that she could not. How then could she be sure if these were the three men who had robbed them, which one she had bitten, and which one threw her companion out of the train? She admitted that she could not be sure but these men had been arrested by the police and she had been asked to identify them. Did she know that the accused, who had

had themselves shaved, had been forced by the police to
grow their beards before she was asked to identify them?
No, she was not aware of that. The identification parade
had been a very shoddy affair. Of the twelve men lined up
before her, only three were bearded Sikhs; she had pointed
them out. She readily admitted that if all of them had been
bearded and turbanned she would have found it very
difficult to spot the guilty. She also admitted that a police
officer had offered to help her identify the accused, but
she had refused his offer. I asked her to look at the three
accused in handcuffs in the dock and point out the one
she had bitten and the two who had thrown her companion
out of the compartment. She would not look at the accused
men. The prosecution counsel and the Judge tried to shout
me down. I stood my ground and insisted that my question
be put on record before the judge decided to rule it out.
The question was recorded. The judge had second thoughts
about ruling it out and very gently asked the witness if she
would care to answer it. The girl broke down crying, 'No,
no, no. I don't want to look at these bloody villains. Please
let me go.' All this was recorded and the girl was helped
out of the court room by two British soldiers. I made my
defence speech to a very irate judge who looked as if he
would have liked to hang me. I left for Lahore, and a few
days later for Kasauli. I learned later that the Sessions Judge
had acquitted all the three accused for lack of convincing
evidence. I had little doubt in my mind that the three men
I had got scot free were guilty of robbery and murder. That
was the sort of thing that nauseated me about the legal
profession. It had very little to do with justice.

* * *

Suddenly riots broke out in Lahore. They were sparked off
by the Sikh leader Master Tara Singh making a
melodramatic gesture outside the Punjab Legislative
Assembly building. Inside the Chamber, the Chief Minister,

Khizar Hayat Tiwana, had succumbed to pressure from the Muslim League and resigned. It was now clear that the Muslims of the Punjab had also opted for Pakistan. As soon as the session was over, Master Tara Singh drew his *kirpan* out of its sheath and yelled *'Pakistan murdabad'* (death to Pakistan). It was like hurling a lighted matchstick into a room full of explosive gas. Communal riots broke out all over the province. Muslims had the upper hand in the killings. They were in the majority, better organized and better motivated than Hindus or Sikhs. The Punjab police was largely Muslim and shamelessly prejudiced in favour of their co-religionists. The only organized group to offer resistance to Muslim gangs was the RSS, but all it could do was to explode a few bombs, killing perhaps one or two people. Then it disappeared from the scene. Urban Sikhs were a pathetic lot. They boasted of their martial prowess (they had none) and waved long *kirpans* they had never wielded before.

One day a Bihari working at a petrol station which I used was knifed to death in broad daylight by two Muslim boys aged eleven and twelve. Unsuspecting Sikhs, riding bicycles, were toppled over by ropes stretched across roads being suddenly raised from either side, and stabbed. Our nights were disturbed by sudden outbursts of cries of *'Allah-o-Akbar'* from one side replied to by *'Sat Sri Akal'* and *'Har Har Mahadev'* from the other. Muslims had more confidence. They would come close to Hindu and Sikh localities and shout *'Hoshiyaar! Shikar ka hai intezaar!'* (Beware, we await our quarry.)

Whatever little resistance Hindus and Sikhs put up against Muslim *goondaism* collapsed one hot afternoon in June 1947. We heard no sounds of gunfire or yelling; we saw only black clouds of smoke billowing out of the city. The entirely Hindu *mohalla* of Shahalmi had been set on fire. Hindus and Sikhs began to leave Lahore, taking whatever they could with them. A few days later, they were forced out without being allowed to take anything. Their homes and belongings were taken over by their Muslim neighbours.

I did not know how long I would be able to stay on in Lahore. I had sent my two small children to their maternal grandparents in Kasauli. My next-door neighbours on either side proclaimed their religious identity on their walls; a large cross on the one side to indicate they were Christians; on the other, big letters in Urdu stating *Parsee ka Makaan* (this is a Parsee home). Close by lived Justice Taja Singh. He had often exhorted me and other Sikhs to stick it out. One morning early in August when I drove up to his house, I found it padlocked. The *chowkidar* told me that his master had left for Delhi. It was my college friend from London days, C. H. Everette, then head of the CID, who advised me to leave Lahore for a few days till the situation returned to normal. 'Leave your home and things in the care of some Muslim friend,' he advised. Manzur was at the time doing some case in Simla. I rang him up and we arranged to meet at Dharampur on the Kalka-Simla road, near where the road to Kasauli branches off. The following night my wife and I and our Hindu cook were escorted by a posse of Baloch policemen provided by Everette to the railway station. We left our young Sikh servant, Dalip Singh, in charge of our house till the Qadirs moved in to look after it. We arrived next morning at Kalka without any untoward incident. I had sent my car ahead to meet us there. We drove up to Dharampur. A few minutes later Manzur arrived by taxi from Simla. He told me that some Kashmiri Muslim labourers had been stabbed in Simla and Muslims were pulling out of Himachal hill resorts. I handed him the keys of my house. We embraced each other. I promised to get back as soon as things were more settled.

We spent some days at Kasauli. By then the mass exodus of Hindus and Sikhs from Pakistan and Muslims from East Punjab had begun. There were gory tales of attacks on trains and road convoys in which thousands were massacred in cold blood. Sikhs who had taken a terrible beating in

West Punjab were out seeking bloody revenge on innocent Muslims of East Punjab, mopping up one Muslim village after another. I decided to run the gauntlet and get to Delhi. I had to make up my mind about what to do. I left my wife and children at Kasauli. I took a motor mechanic with me in the event of the car giving trouble. Some miles beyond Kalka I discovered that petrol stations along the road were closed. I returned to Kalka to fill up the tank and take a spare can of petrol. On the way I found our servant Dalip Singh walking along the road. He told me that Muslim mobs had come to the house. The Qadirs and their servants had hidden him in an attic for several days. Manzur had removed my name from the gate and put up his own in its place. However, word had leaked out that a Sikh was being given shelter and *goondas* wanted to search the house. Manzur was able to get the police just in time to prevent them breaking in. That night he put Dalip Singh in the boot of his car and drove him to the new Indo-Pak border. He gave him money and instructed him to board a train going from Amritsar to Kalka. That is how he came to be there. Not having heard of Kasauli, the fellow had taken the road to Delhi hoping to catch a bus somewhere on the way.

I put Dalip Singh in the car, took enough petrol to get us to Delhi, and proceeded on my way. There was not a soul on the road, no sign of life in any of the towns or villages through which we passed. It was only after I had passed Karnal, some sixty miles short of Delhi, that I saw a jeep coming towards me. I pulled up. So did the jeep, about a hundred yards from me. I took out my pistol and waited. After an agonizing five minutes of staring at the jeep, I noticed that its occupants were Sikhs. Two men stepped out on the road with rifles in their hands. I felt reassured and drove up to the jeep. I asked them if it was safe to proceed to Delhi. 'Quite safe,' they assured me. 'We have killed the lot in villages along the road.' They used the word *sooar* (pig) for Muslims. It churned my stomach. This was no place to argue with them.

I arrived safely in Delhi, a few days before India was to be declared independent. I had my father's home to go to. Hundreds of thousands of others who like me had fled Pakistan had nowhere to go. Some were housed in refugee camps; others occupied old monuments, railway station platforms, or verandas outside shops and offices, or made their homes on pavements.

The magnitude of the tragedy that had taken place was temporarily drowned in the euphoria of the Independence to come. It was like a person who feels no hurt when his arm or leg is suddenly cut off: the pain comes after some time.

On the night of 14 August, I joined the stream of humanity moving towards Parliament House. With me was my wife's cousin, Harji Malik. We managed to get to the Parliament by 11 p.m. The throng was immense disciplined, and full of enthusiasm. Periodically it burs into cries of *'Mahatma Gandhi ki jai'* and *'Inquilab zindabad* A minute before the midnight hour a hush of silenc spread over the crowd. The voice of Sucheta Kripalan singing *'Bande Mataram'* came over the loud-speakers. I was followed by Pandit Nehru making his memorable speech: 'Long years ago we made a tryst with destiny...Now comes the time to redeem that pledge...' and so on. As the speech ended, the crowd burst into cheers and yelling of slogans. We embraced strangers and congratulated each other for having gained our freedom. We did not get home till after 2 a.m.

I was up early to be able to get to the Red Fort to see the Union Jack come down and the Indian tricolour go up. Once again the whole route was crowded with people going on foot. Lord and Lady Mountbatten drove up in their six-horsed Viceregal carriage. The horses were unharnessed. The people decided to pull the carriage with their own hands. Many British officers were picked up and carried by the crowd on their shoulders. Almost overnight the much-hated English had become the Indians' most-loved foreigners.

I stood about fifty yards away from the ramparts of the Red Fort. I heard the buglers sound the 'Last Post' as Lord Mountbatten lowered the Union Jack. I heard the band play the National Anthem *Jana Gana Mana'* as Pandit Nehru hoisted the Indian tricolour. I heard the canons roar to salute the new President of the Republic. I heard all but saw very little because tears of joy blurred my vision. And my heart was full of pride.

Akhtar Payami

Akhtar Payami is a veteran journalist and writer. He is also a poet, his long poem *Tareekh* has been published across the border and a collection of his poems is in press.

Born in 1930 in Patna, Bihar he was educated at Gaya, Calcutta and Ranchi. He did his Bachelors in Applied Economics from the Patna University and edited the Urdu weekly *Nai Manzil* during the crucial Partition years. In 1951 he migrated to Dhaka, where after some teaching assignments he joined the *Morning News*. He wrote its last editorial which appeared on 16 December 1971 —the day Pakistan was dismembered.

After the emergence of Bangladesh he worked as chief editor for the newly formed Eastern News Agency (ENA) based in Dhaka.

In 1972, Akhtar Payami migrated to Pakistan along with his family. Their route to Karachi was rather circuitous and they encountered several difficulties in the course of their travels.

In Karachi he rejoined the *Morning News* and was associated with it till the late seventies. In 1980, he joined the *Dawn* and has been working with the newspaper in various capacities ever since.

Then and Now

Akhtar Payami

In a vast sea of humanity a frail, barely-clothed, bespectacled old man sat on a rostrum. He had been on hunger strike for several days to protest against the continued killing of human beings in a spate of communal frenzy in Calcutta. The plan for the bifurcation of the subcontinent had been announced. In a couple of days the sun was to set finally on the British Empire and two independent states were to come into existence.

The mammoth crowd on the *maïdan* had transcended all barriers. Hindus, Muslims, Sikhs, Christians, and a host of other minorities had congregated at one place. There was no animosity, no ill-feeling, no hatred, and no fear. It was a unique assembly of diverse people having different faiths. They had come from far-off places with a pledge never to indulge in any killing spree. They were requesting the distinguished hunger-striker to break his fast.

Along with him on the raised platform was an energetic, enlightened, and mercurial leader with a glass of orange juice in his hand. At long last he had been able to persuade the ascetic to break his fast unto death. Suhrawardy's politics of persuasion yielded results. Gandhi ended his hunger strike. The anxious people who had gathered there to watch this dramatic event heaved a sigh of relief. (Gandhi lived a few more years, only to meet a violent death. He was assassinated by a militant protagonist of Hindu revivalism. Suhrawardy, who later became Prime Minister of Pakistan, was found dead in a Beirut hotel in mysterious circumstances.)

That was perhaps the last inspiring spectacle of unity that the subcontinent witnessed at a time when major changes were taking place in many parts of the world. Only a few days earlier, communal passions had been running high. People were frightened of their own shadows. Few ventured to get out of their houses. Death lay in ambush.

In those days of heightened tension, I, along with some close friends, proceeded to a court to seek permission to bring out an Urdu journal. This was a legal requirement for publishing a newspaper or a magazine. Suddenly it started raining heavily. We spotted an elderly man walking briskly with an umbrella. As we approached him to take shelter under his umbrella, he looked at us with suspicion. His piercing eyes scrutinized us to identify our 'religious status'. Convinced of the risk involved, he muttered, 'your motive seems to be bad,' and walked away hastily. In those days far too many cases of stabbing were being reported every day. Later, we had a hearty laugh at the nervous behaviour of the old man. How could he ever know that he was meeting different creatures who did not have any ill motive against anyone?

That was Calcutta on the eve of independence.

Founded by an official of the East India Company in 1690 on an eighty-mile tract of land gifted by the ruler of Bengal, this city, by the end of the eighteenth century, had turned into a formidable 'economic powerhouse' and the capital of the Company's government. Who could even dream at that time that after nearly 250 years, Calcutta would assume a new hospitable character, drawing people from all over the country? It was here that people from all over India would trek to find jobs. Most of them stayed there by themselves, leaving their families behind at distant places. They worked hard to earn their livelihood and returned to their kith and kin only during festivals.

The port city presented a unique contrast. Being the main power-centre of the East India Company, a precisely demarcated part of Calcutta where the rulers lived in luxury and abundance wore a mini-London look. On special occasions it almost turned into a dreamland, where gala parties were held with food and drinks imported from Europe. The roads leading to the venue of such extravaganzas were lighted with double rows of lamps on each side. The gardens were illuminated with thousands of coloured lamps. Experts in firework displays were brought down from all over the country to demonstrate their skill. The guests appeared in fancy dresses. Tables were laid with delicious food prepared by famous French cooks. Different bands of martial music were in attendance in several parts of the gardens.

As opposed to this exhibition of high living, Calcutta also presented a scattered and confused chaos of houses, huts, sheds, lanes, windings, and alleys. There was an undistinguishable mass of filth and corruption, equally offensive to human sense and health. It was this part of the East Indian Company's capital that had a cosmopolitan character. It was here that people, irrespective of their caste, creed, colour, lived—and lived peacefully.

The upper strata of society easily and eagerly associated themselves with the rulers in the pursuit of power and pelf. They lived their lives with borrowed pride and prejudices. But this motley crowd did not represent the heart of India. There were countless others, coming from all parts of the country. And Calcutta, like an affectionate mother, welcomed all of them with open arms and without any discrimination whatsoever. Although politics stealthily crept into the inner recesses of society, demolishing old traditions and values, there was an unwritten accord and understanding among the people to co-exist in all circumstances. It was a common concern, a shared yearning for a better life, that united them. The social environment had not been polluted by narrow considerations.

Towards the closing days of the Raj, when Calcutta was emerging as an industrial city, workers and labourers from all over India collected there in search of a living. As most of them came from an exploited class, their common target of attack was the exploitative system. By that time the trade union movement had started taking root in the changing industrial environment of India. Irrespective of their religious beliefs, the workers had a common perception of problems and struggled collectively for their solution.

But gradually, with the rise of communal politics and the narrow approach and gross miscalculations of political leaders, a political divide on communal lines began to take shape. Calcutta started losing the race of endurance. Educational institutions were set up on a communal basis. Sports groups were formed on a similar pattern. Areas were demarcated for the settlement of the two communities. A sense of unexplained fear started gripping the erstwhile happy and contented population of Calcutta.

In spite of these divisive trends, what remained indivisible was the cultural unity and intellectual exuberance of the people. They continued to derive inspiration from the same unpolluted source. Writers, poets, intellectuals, thinkers, artists, and painters formed an island of peace and inspiration in a sea of rising hatred. But this small minority could not for long outface the avalanche that politics had unleashed across the country.

* * *

If Bengal was a symbol of cultural unity, the adjoining province of Bihar had a similar story to narrate.

Many people might not know that it was Bihar where the first extended empire of the subcontinent was formed in 326 BC, with Patliputra, the site of modern Patna, as the capital. The splendour and sophistication of Chandragupta's empire is revealed in the detailed accounts of court life by Megasthenes, the Greek ambassador to the Patliputra Court.

Chandragupta's grandson, Ashoka, says in one of his rock edicts: 'There is verily no duty which is more important to me than promoting the welfare of all men.' This humane approach, derived mainly from the teachings of Buddha, continued to dominate the socio-cultural life of Bihar for a long time.

Although the Muslims formed a small percentage of the population, there was a cultural harmony among the people. This harmony was witnessed not only at the intellectual level. Certain widely-accepted social norms were equally respected by all sections of society. Hindus and Muslims used to visit each other on social occasions. They attended each other's religious ceremonies. During Eid-ul-Fitr and Holi delightful spectacles of cultural unity were visible. At many places, particularly in the rural areas, ceremonies were attended by members of various religious groups. They mingled with each other without any mental reservations. Though merciless historical factors had started eroding the feeling of oneness, some elements of higher considerations were still valued by many people. If there was a bereavement in a neighbour's family, notwithstanding his religious beliefs, people would visit him to express sympathy. They consoled him sincerely and shared his sorrow.

Fundamentalism till then was an alien concept. Orthodox Muslims and Hindus performed their religious rites with devotion and dedication. But religion never stood in their way in discharging social responsibilities. Hindus and Muslims jointly attended marriage ceremonies and actively participated in rejoicings. It is true that separate arrangements had to be made for their meals, but this never created any problems for the hosts. The Muslims usually had their food on some kind of plates. The Hindus were generally served food on banana leaves or the leaves of some other plants. The cooks were naturally not common. Drinking water was offered in glasses made of clay which could be discarded immediately after use. Despite such visible differences in social behaviour a spirit of understanding prevailed everywhere. It largely dominated the conduct of the members of the two communities.

In rural areas where the Muslims were in a microscopic minority, a number of customs and traditions were readily accepted and practised in Muslim households. The memory of a festival known as 'Swarswati Puja', celebrated to pay homage to the Hindu goddess of learning, comes to mind. Young students playing with small sticks and chanting verses moved in concert in their localities and into each other's houses without any sense of regimentation. The children were offered gifts in cash or kind by the elders of society. No Muslim, howsoever orthodox in his views, ever thought that by joining such celebrations, their children would be influenced by Hindu mythology. The Hindu goddess, obviously, did not exercise any corrupting influence on them.

* * *

The rigidity that formed the hallmark of Hinduism was not shared by all Hindus. In the aftermath of a high tide of liberalism that swept India through the writings of social reformers like Raja Ram Mohan Roy, many Hindus started having serious doubts about a religion that is discriminatory in nature. They were critical of the traditional concept of the 'Untouchables', and of the low status of women that Hinduism preached and practised. Along with this, they also started reviewing the notion that held the Muslims to be usurpers of their rights. True, such people were few and far between. They belonged to the educated and enlightened sections of society. But they did exercise considerable influence on others. An educated middle class was emerging fast, with a different notion of social relationship.

Such views were reinforced and strengthened by the movements launched by political parties and groups having liberal views. Founded on a different basis, and representing a class structure of their own, they could not afford to indulge in the luxury of identifying themselves with any particular faith. For them there was no difference between a Hindu labourer and a Muslim labourer. Some progressive peasant movements too did not discriminate between a Muslim farmer and a Hindu farmer. Such political parties and groups had limited areas of operation. But their leaders and followers generally had a non-communal outlook. They had no prejudices. Religion did not prevent them from launching a united struggle against the outdated and highly-discriminatory land-tenure system. Among the notable peasant leaders of those days were Swami Sahjanand of Bihar and Haji Mohammad Danish of Bengal. But unfortunately their pull was not strong enough to sustain their movement and stop the mighty waves of communal passion. The political climate, already vitiated by that time, was consistently driving a wedge between the two major communities.

The Communist Party of India, which spearheaded the left movement in the subcontinent, made a major departure from its stand on national politics. Convinced of the ultimate division of the country on a communal basis, it directed its Muslim and Hindu cadres to work separately in areas where their presence would not be questioned. The Muslim cadres were asked to visit Muslim labourers and peasants, and the Hindu cadres were advised to educate Hindu workers and farmers as they would listen to them without any reservations. This significant digression from a non-communal approach to the country's politics expressly indicated the approaching collapse of communal harmony. Political parties and groups and social and cultural organizations started assuming a communal complexion. While the higher echelons of society maintained a facade of unity and understanding, the seeds of hatred and animosity were quietly taking root. Distrust, misgivings, and lack of faith in old and traditionally-accepted moral values had started appearing in the forefront of social behaviour.

* * *

In his book, *The Autobiography of an Unknown Indian,* Nirad C. Chaudhri mentions four distinct aspects of the attitude of the Hindus towards the Muslims: hostility for their one-time domination of the Hindus; total indifference to the Muslims as an element in contemporary society; the nurture and practice of friendliness for Muslims of their own economic and social status; mixed concern and contempt for the Muslim peasants, who were seen in the same light as the low-caste Hindu tenants.

Nirad Chaudhri recalls that in nineteenth-century Bengali literature the Muslims were always referred to under the contemptuous epithet of *yavana.* The historical romances of Bankim Chatterji and Ramesh Chandra Dutt glorified Hindu rebellion against the Muslims. Throughout the nineteenth century, Hindu culture was taken back to its ancient Sanskrit traditions. The only non-Hindu influence which it recognized and tried to assimilate was European. All thinkers and reformers of modern India, from Raja Ram Mohan Roy to Rabindra Nath Tagore, according to him, based their life-work on the formula of a synthesis of Hindu and European currents. Islamic trends and traditions did not touch even the 'arc of their consciousness'.

Nirad Chaudhri may have had his own reasons for being so blunt about the genesis of a sharply-deteriorating communal situation in India. But his analysis may not be wholly objective or correct. While Bankim Chatterji and a few others did write with venom, there were many others who did not share their views. Tagore, for instance, cannot be accused of preaching hatred. Glorification of the past does not necessarily imply rejection of the present.

* * *

Whenever there is a major political upheaval in any part of the world, truth is the first casualty. Expediencies and personal considerations banish objectivity. Facts are distorted to substantiate arguments in support of a specific point of view. Precisely this happened with issues relating to the division of the subcontinent. The fact remains that acrimony and animosity reached a peak where it was almost impossible for the Hindus and the Muslims to trust each other. But this trend, gleefully nurtured by wild and vicious political propagandists, could not falsify history. Despite certain aberrations, the two communities had developed a pattern of relationship based on the concept of co-existence.

Digging into the past may not be a rewarding exercise today. Nevertheless, it is never too late to make sincere efforts to analyse a course of events that had a tremendous bearing on history. In doing so an objective assessment of the situation is absolutely necessary. Some people may be tempted to restructure history and recreate facts to strengthen their contentions. But such temptations must be spurned in the interest of truth and justice.

* * *

Nobody can deny that several parallel currents representing various shades of opinion were in existence in undivided India. At certain levels, guided by motives of self-preservation, one community nourished and demonstrated intolerance towards the other community. But otherwise, there were also inspiring examples of human relationships of the highest order that bound them together. In the area of personal relationships and in the sphere of performing arts, there were many instances to refute the allegations that the Muslims suffered from a deep feeling of alienation. Hindu and Muslim neighbours lived peacefully and offered their services to each other whenever needed. Similarly in the promotion of art and literature, they worked together.

Urdu till then was not condemned as the language of the invaders. In fact, it used to be regarded as an integral part of a distinct culture. Collections of many classical poets were brought out by Hindu publishers. Most notable among them was the Nawal Kishore Press, which printed those books with great care. Elegies of Meer Anees and his contemporaries were also published by Munshi Nawal Kishore. Among the writers of great fame and accomplishment both Mohammad Hussain Azad and Ratan Nath Sarshar occupied a coveted place. Among a large number of distinguished poets were Daya Shankar Naseem, Brij Narayan Chakbast, Pundit Hari Chandra Akhtar, Raghupati Sahay, Firaq Gorakhpuri, Anand Narayan Mulla, and a host of others. The value of their writings was not assessed with reference to their faith.

In Gaya, a district town of Bihar, there were a number of Hindu poets of Urdu whose knowledge and understanding of the language was remarkable. Awadh Kumar, Kushta Gayavi, Jugeshwar Prasad, and Khalish, were lawyers by profession but their commitment to Urdu was unquestionable. Astonishing was their comprehension of Urdu and its nuances. Not only did they compose poems in Urdu, triumphantly they recited their poems at *mushairas*. The audience, consisting mainly of Urdu-speakers, applauded them without restraint. With their meagre resources, they also made considerable contributions towards organizing functions for the promotion of Urdu. Even in religious and reverential literature, largely dominated by Muslims, Hindus had a prominent place. Nanak Lakhnavi recited his *mersia* sitting on a rostrum in Muharram *majalis*. His venture was never treated as a trespass and never questioned by any section of society.

A slow but perceptible change was, however, taking place in the country. Some Hindu intellectuals believed that their attitude to the Muslims was influenced, if not by positive utterances, at all events by the 'silences' of their nineteenth-century writers. They thought that in those writers the hatred of the Muslim was 'the hatred of the Muslim in history'. The concept of Indian nationalism, to a great extent, was marked by a conscious effort to distance the Hindus from everything that had a Muslim imprint. Some Hindu writers unreservedly supported Bepin Chandra Pal, a major theoretician of the Swadeshi Movement, who said, 'if the Moslem leaders tried to wipe out the memories of the Sikhs and the Marathas, the Hindu nationalist leaders sought to revive them'. He claimed that it was a 'supreme psychological need of the nationalist propaganda'.

* * *

When it became much too evident that after the Second World War the British would be left with no option but to transfer power to the Indians, the Hindu-Muslim rivalry assumed new dimensions. The Muslim League had been formed in 1906, and since then the Hindus had started developing a new sense of hatred for the Muslims. This change in their attitude adversely affected the personal relationship between Hindu and Muslim families who had lived together for decades without any major friction. Communal clashes took place in Comilla (now in Bangladesh) on the visit of Nawab Sir Salimullah, at whose residence the Muslim League was formed. This was followed by a similar incident in Jamalpur, a subdivisional headquarter of Mymensingh (also in Bangladesh). Thus the seed of alienation was quietly sown. Posterity was to do the harvesting.

It appears that while the 'politics of the extreme' was taking root in Indian soil, nobody, not even the renowned protagonists of unity, made any visible or invisible move to protect the frontiers of their idealism.

With the passage of time the two communities further hardened their political positions. They suddenly discovered a large number of issues that separated them from others. Those issues were blown up out of proportion. The past was conveniently ignored. The present, shrouded in clouds of distrust and misapprehension, was accepted as the prime reality. In the heat of a wild frenzy, nobody had the time or the inclination to think beyond a circumscribed vision.

To substantiate the preconceived notion that the Muslims did not contribute to the formulation of a common thinking, it is sometimes argued that the Muslims did not derive any inspiration from the mighty Himalayas or the benevolent Ganges. The fact, however, remains that Urdu literature is filled with instances that show how Muslim poets and writers eulogized these symbols of grandeur.

A casual look at the physiognomy of the Indians clearly reveals that all of them do not belong to one ethnic stock. They are derived from Aryans, Dravidians, and a host of unidentified aboriginal tribes, with a sprinkling of Mongols, Greeks, Scythians, Huns, Arabs, Turks, Afghans, and Ceylonese, along with some Chinese, Indonesians, and even Ethiopeans. All these groups have, from time to time, injected their blood into the mainstream, thereby creating a complex multicoloured and multiracial kaleidoscopic picture.

It is a tragic reality that this kaleidoscopic picture started fading when tension mounted. Justice G. D. Khosla, in his book entitled *Stern Reckoning,* says:

Madness swept over the entire land, in the ever-increasing crescendo, till reason and sanity left the minds of rational men and women, and sorrow and misery, hatred, despair took possession of their soul. A Sikh or a Hindu dared not show his face in the place where he and his forefathers had lived for centuries, and a Muslim was forced to abandon his native soil, his home and his property.

In all societies there are bound to be individuals who will commit crimes against others. They will assault, beat up, torture, maim, or murder other people. They will steal, rob, or misappropriate the property of others. It was in this context that a major political leader confessed, 'there are nasty Hindus as there are nasty Mussalmans who would pick a quarrel for nothing'.

During the traumatic period of Partition, many Muslims had, at great risk to themselves and their families, given shelter to Hindus. There are examples of some Muslims doing so in almost every communal riot. Some Muslims have actually suffered great losses and have even faced death in their effort to offer protection to Hindus. Many Hindus, too, have bravely faced threats and dangers in their determination to save the life and property of Muslims.

A survey conducted by a British author gave a different picture of the Hindu-Muslim relationship. Many Hindus admitted that there were millions of Muslims who were as tender-hearted as the noblest Brahmin could hope to be. As against this, according to the survey, there were millions of Hindus who, right from their early childhood, were aggressive, violent, ill-tempered, and cruel individuals.

While all such variations form the mosaic of life, one thing is certain: nothing brings two individuals or two groups closer than the sharing of each other's sorrows.

B.K. (Braj Kumar) Nehru

Civil servant and barrister *par excellence;* born on 4 September 1909 in Allahabad, he acquired choice academic credentials at the London School of Economics, Balliol College, Oxford, and the Inner Temple, London.

B.K. Nehru's record of public service is an impressive list of achievements over a period of sixty years. He joined the ICS in 1934, and served in important administrative posts in District Management and the Ministry of Finance. He represented India on numerous international platforms including the Reparations Conference, 1945, the Commonwealth Finance Ministers' Conference, the UN General Assembly 1949-52 and in 1960, the FAO Conferences 1949-50, Sterling Balances Conferences 1947-9, and the Bandung Conference, 1955. He was a member of the UN Advisory Committee on Administrative and Budgetary Questions 1951-3, and the UN Investment Committee 1962, for which he was also Chairperson 1977-91, and member emeritus 1991. He served as Ambassador in Washington 1961-8, and as High Commissioner in London 1973-7. B.K. Nehru was Executive Director of the IBRD (World Bank) 1949-54 and 1958-62. He was deputed to enquire into Australian Federal Finance 1946, invited to be an adviser to the government of Sudan 1955, and was the Vice-President of the Vienna Institute of Development 1962-87.

He has been awarded honorary degrees from several universities, and takes a keen interest in philanthropic works. His publications are: *Australian Federal Finance,* 1947; *Speaking of India,* 1966, and *Thoughts on the Present Discontents,* 1986. He lives in Kasauli, and enjoys bridge, reading, and conversation.

Memories of a Shared Culture

B. K. Nehru

The structure of Indian society before independence was based more on class than on religion or caste. The higher one ranked in the hierarchy, the less did religion or caste matter; it was class that counted. The class structure itself was, as in most old societies, based on the possession of land. At the top of the social dung heap were, of course, the 'native' princes. Till the first Gandhian onslaught on the citadel of British power after Jallianwalla Bagh, all Indians were 'natives' irrespective of rank.

Next in the hierarchy came the large landowners—the *zamindars* and *taluqdars*. There were no limits to the size of land holdings as there are today, and the size of the larger estates was enormous. These large landlords were often dignified with titles that were otherwise reserved for the ruling princes; they were often described as Rajas and sometimes even as Maharajas, irrespective of their religion. The estates were sometimes so large that officers of the ICS were lent to these barons to manage their properties. A fellow student of mine was asked at the viva voce for the ICS how much land his family owned. He said he did not know in terms of acres, but it owned 300 villages!

As the landlords' income was from agriculture, it was then, as now, free of income tax. The owner of the land did, however, have to pay land revenue which, though in most areas it was revised periodically, was not at all high. Not content, however, with their legitimate incomes—and always short of cash—these gentlemen levied on their unfortunate ryots all kinds of illegal exactions—*shadiana* to pay for a wedding in the family, *hathiana* to buy an elephant, or *motorana* if the Raja desired another automobile! It was on the loyalty of the princes and these enormously rich landlords, whose wealth and prosperity were dependent entirely on the goodwill of the government, that the British relied for support in the continuance of their rule. As a quid pro quo for this support, not only the ruling princes but these barons too were allowed to do all they liked with their subjects and their tenantry.

Next in the social hierarchy came the professional classes. These consisted at that time essentially of lawyers, doctors, and members of the 'Imperial Services' headed by the ICS. The senior members of the ICS were, however, at the very top—even above the ruling princes. The men at the top of the legal profession, such as Pandit Motilal Nehru or Sir Tej Bahadur Sapru in Allahabad, the Imam brothers, Sir Ali and Sir Hasan in Patna, Sir Mohammed Shafi in Lahore, had colossal incomes that came largely from the quarrels amongst each other of the landed gentry. Quite literally, having nothing to do after the desires of the flesh had been satisfied, their favourite pastime was to engage in a contest of one-upmanship with each other. Another major source of the lawyers' income was the continuous friction between the Government of India and the Princes. The former was forever trying to increase its role; the latter were forever resisting it. The advice of lawyers was always necessary, and it was very expensive! The leading doctors like Dr B. C. Roy in Calcutta and Hakim Ajmal Khan in Delhi also enjoyed this kind of income, for no expense was spared to restore the physiques which continuous abuse had damaged.

The Imperial Services, in particular the ICS, enjoyed their position at the top of the social scale not by virtue of their wealth, which (though they were very well-paid) was far from that of the Princes or the landed gentry but by virtue of their power. The members of the Political Service recruited from the ICS and the Indian Army, from which came the Residents and Political Agents at the courts of the Ruling Princes, literally held their thrones in their hands. The ICS, which provided the Governors of the Provinces and, earlier on exclusively, the members of the Executive Councils of the Governors as well as of the Viceroy, together with the officers of the entire senior administration, held in their hands the fate of the landed aristocracy.

At the very bottom of the social scale, but excluded from the Establishment, were those who called themselves bankers, but whom others called money-lenders. They too were rich, but wealth derived from such lowly practices as money-lending or trading or shop-keeping had no place at all in the social hierarchy. Bulaki Shah of Lahore, who may still be remembered there by people of my generation, was very rich, but it was unthinkable that he would ever be invited into the drawing-room of even the most junior member of the ICS with a salary of no more than Rs 450 per month.

Beyond the landed gentry and the professionals, there was really nothing. There was no large-scale industry worth the name, nor large-scale commerce—which enabled the new rich in Britain to break the monopoly on political power of the landed gentry in the nineteenth century— except in Bombay and Bengal, where indigenous industry was struggling to establish itself.

The result was that between these very rich and not so rich but very powerful members of the Establishment and the rest of the people there was an enormous gap. As I look back into my childhood, the definition of 'people' was 'people like us'; the vast majority of the people of India did not, in the thinking of the Establishment, come into consideration at all. Even as late as the 1930s, when the Indian National Congress had, under the leadership of Gandhi, long been hijacked by the common man, the Establishment was still not concerned with his fate. Their own economic wants having been satisfied—and more than satisfied—the subject of 'economics' was not considered worthy of attention by people of such exalted stature. It was only *banias* and *muneems* who polluted their minds with thoughts of pelf.

To illustrate this attitude of disdain among the upper classes for the lowly subject of lucre, I shall relate an incident which remains impressed on my mind. The nineteen thirties were, because of the world-wide recession, a time of acute economic hardship for the people of India, to remove whose poverty was in any case one of the prime objectives of the independence struggle. The Rt. Hon. M. R. Jayakar, a distinguished Liberal leader, was addressing the Indian students in Cambridge. He had waxed eloquent about the various demands he had put forward to the British Government at the Round Table Conference then in session in London about what the new Indian Constitution should contain. A student (if I remember rightly it was none other than the subsequently-famous Rehmat Ali) asked him what the economic situation in India was like. He said, 'You see, I am not an economics man.' Then he went on to say, very gravely, 'But I can tell you the economic situation is very bad. It is very difficult to get a servant in Bombay!'

Within this elite there was no difference based on religion or caste. In it religion was irrelevant; there was virtually a complete identity of culture. Its members lived the same way, they ate more or less the same food, they wore the same clothes, they spoke the same language and had the same interests. This was true of the Establishment all over India, though the contents of the common culture naturally varied with geography according to local history and environment.

The roots of this common culture lay in the Mughal courts—those of the Emperor and his provincial satraps—from which the Establishment itself was descended. The court dress, the etiquette, the music, the dances, the arts, the amusements and pastimes, and the food were all variants of those of the Mughal court.

So powerful was the influence of the court of the Emperor that even the courts of the rebels who destroyed the Empire—the courts of the Peshwa and the Maratha princes—followed the protocol, the rituals, the procedure, and the etiquette of the Court at Delhi. The court language of the Mughals was Persian. All the languages of the country, particularly of the north, were penetrated by Persian as, during the British Raj, and even today, they are being penetrated by English. All had an admixture of Persian words. None of them, however, adopted the Persian script, with the sole exception of Hindi, which was written both in the Devanagari and the Persian scripts. That language written in the Persian script gradually developed into a separate language known as Urdu.

Inevitably this culture had a large Islamic content. The 'common culture', the *mushtarika tahzeeb* which we so fondly remember today both in India and Pakistan, was the culture of this already effete Establishment. Cultures are most enjoyable in their decadent phase; that is why we of the erstwhile Establishment look back on our culture of pre-Independence days with such nostalgia.

It was into this Establishment that I was born. Motilal Nehru, the head of the family, being a lawyer with a huge practice, belonged very much to the Establishment. His life-style, until the non-co-operation movement of 1920, was therefore very much the same as that of the great *taluqdars* of Oudh. My life as a student was split between Allahabad and Lahore, from which city came my mother, whose father, Raja Narendra Nath, was triply a member of the Establishment, being not only the scion of an aristocratic family but a Civil Servant and a large landowner to boot. I had, therefore, ample opportunity of witnessing the kind of life that was lived by the elite in pre-independence and pre-partition India, and later on of living it myself, though in a very considerably modified form, as a member of the Indian Civil Service.

One of the striking features of this life was that, unlike what happened during a short time before partition, one was never conscious at all of the religion of one's friends. This was particularly true of both the Nehru and the Narendra Nath families. We were Kashmiri Pandits whose ancestral profession was the Civil Service. As the dominant culture of the Mughal courts was Islamic, the life-style of the Kashmiri Pandits, who were very much a part of the court culture, was naturally greatly affected by that of their Muslim counterparts. The education of the elite till almost the end of the nineteenth century had a Persian and Arabic base. Raja Narendra Nath was a considerable scholar in both languages. He was soaked in Islamic culture, being almost a *hafiz* of the Koran. Though he was in later life the President of the Hindu Mahasaba, it was the religion of Islam which he admired and not Hinduism. His admiration for Islam was so great that he found nothing wrong with it at all; for Hinduism as a religion he did not, on the contrary, have any use. The explanation for his being the President of the Hindu Mahasabha was that he was a political Hindu and not a religious one. Similarly, Pandit Motilal Nehru was also educated in Arabic and Persian, though his knowledge of these languages was by no means as profound as that of my maternal grandfather. Nor did he have any great knowledge of, or interest in, Islam. He was very much a rationalist, and to him all religions including Hinduism were equally damnable.

Added on to this background of Islamic culture was modernization which, at that time in India, and even now to a considerable extent, meant westernization and anglicization. The Nehrus were highly westernized, in both their mode of living and their modes of thought. My maternal family lived more in the Indian style but its thinking and its values were equally western. The result of this background was that in both family homes, as in the home of my parents, what I observed was a complete absence of any consciousness about the religion of those with whom one came into contact. The Maharaja of Mahmudabad and the Raja of Jehangirabad among the great *taluqdars* were great friends of Pandit Motilal Nehru; a particular favourite among them was Thakur (later Raja) Nawab Ali. In the later years the character of the visitors to 'Anand Bhawan' of course changed, but their religious composition never did. Rafi Ahmed Kidwai was as great a friend as Govind Ballabh Pant, and if Pandit Madan Mohan Malaviya or Lala Lajpat Rai came, so also did the Maulanas Mohammed Ali and Shaukat Ali, as well as Maulana Abul Kalam Azad, Hakim Ajmal Khan, Dr Ansari, and Asaf Ali.

The most trusted and highest-ranking member of the staff was Munshi Mubarak Ali, whom I well remember, a venerable old gentleman with a great white beard who was reputed to be a descendant of the Mughal Emperor and who had a large cottage in the compound. His son Manzar Ali Sokhta, who was of the same age group as my father and Jawaharlal, was brought up and educated in exactly the same fashion as they were and became a lawyer and a junior to Pandit Motilal Nehru in his practice. (The only discrimination was that unlike these two boys he was not sent to England for education.) Manna Bhai, as we children all knew him, was as much a member of the Nehru family as any blood relation, lived for many years with my uncle, and died in a village serving the peasantry as a devout follower of Mahatma Gandhi, working for their betterment.

On the maternal side, the catholicity of the Raja's friendships was equal. I remember well that frequent visitors to the house were Allama Iqbal, Sir Jogender Singh, and Sir Zulfiqar Ali Khan of Malerkotla. These names I specially mention because of their being mentioned in Iqbal's poem *Khamoshi*, which begins with,

Kaisi patey ki baat Jogender ne kal kahi:
Motor hai Zulfiqar Ali Khan ki kya khamosh

Another friend and frequent visitor was, to give him his full title, Lt.-Gen. the Hon. Nawab Sir Ummar Hayat Khan Tiwana, probably the largest landowner and certainly the most powerful member of the Punjab aristocracy because of his leadership of the Tiwana clan (I doubt if many of my readers in Pakistan would know that not all Tiwanas are Muslim; there are plenty of Hindu Tiwanas, now of course all in India). Sir Fazl-i-Hussain, a political opponent, was a personal friend; so was Sir Sikandar Hayat Khan, also a political opponent and a more intimate friend. But what is interesting to note as an example of the class structure of society as it existed then was that, while these political opponents were always welcome in the house, their Hindu colleague and perhaps the most important Minister in Sikandar Hayat's Cabinet, Sir Chhotu Ram, did not have any personal equation with my grandfather. In this household too, the most trusted and important member of the staff was a Muslim. He was the manager of all the Raja's estates, the *Daroga Saheb*, Ali Bakhsh by name, a man of old-world charm, manners, and elegance. It is of interest that one of the most brilliant financial experts of Pakistan, Anwar Ali, brought up in the household and a close friend, was his son.

The list of friends of, and visitors to, the Raja was not limited to the members of the recognized Establishment. Men of learning, of whatever religion, Christian, Muslim, Hindu, or Sikh, or of no religion at all, were equally welcome. One of the conversations which I still remember involved a Maulana quoting an *Aayat* of the Quran to make some point; this was countered by Raja Narendra Nath saying, 'Yes, yes, but go on and finish the *Aayat.*'

Religious taboos were scrupulously respected. No Muslim of good family ever ate beef; no Hindu ate pig meat. When my maternal uncle, Dewan Anand Kumar, returned from Cambridge, he brought back a taste for bacon and eggs for breakfast. Bacon entered the house for the first time. All went well till Khera, an old Muslim family retainer, found out. He went straight to the young Dewan Sahib and told him that he and his ancestors had served the family for four generations, but nobody had ever committed the sacrilege that the future head of the family was now committing, and he had better stop disgracing the family name. This was done forthwith; the side of bacon was taken a furlong away to the furthermost limits of the compound, where it was ceremoniously buried. The poor Dewan Saheb had to wait for the partition of India and to become a refugee before he could indulge once again in his favourite breakfast.

Nor did the Muslims object in those days, as they subsequently very strongly did, to the idiotic Hindu rules about the ritual pollution of food. Food touched by a Muslim was polluted for the orthodox Hindu. But so it was, they knew, if it was touched by anybody but a high-caste Hindu. For the orthodox Kashmiri Pandit even this was not good enough: the person who cooked their food had to be a Kashmir Brahmin. For some Hindus all Kashmiri Pandits were themselves polluted for they were meat-eaters. One of the most intimate friends of my parents was Rama Kant Malaviya, son of the renowned Madan Mohan. He used to live opposite our house in Allahabad and used to spend hours every day in our home. But he could not eat anything touched by us or in our house. We were not only Brahmins but high-class Sarasvat Brahmins at that. But we were meat-eaters and, therefore, ritually unclean. If he ever wanted a drink of water, it was sent for from his own house!

The westernization of these elite families increased the irrelevance of religion: my maternal uncle's best friends were a man called Mohammed Shafi and the well-known Afzal Hussain, brother of Sir Fazli, both of whom were with him at Cambridge. Nor did this non-communal approach to life by our class of people end with that generation. It continued and indeed was strengthened in mine. Till my father's generation, there were no inter-communal marriages; even inter-caste marriages were a rarity. But in my generation this ban was broken. In the Nehru family itself I led the way by marrying a Jew. My cousin Shyma Kumari Nehru married Jamil Khan of the Rampur family, a cousin of the long-serving Foreign Minister of Pakistan, Sahebzada Yakub Khan. Indira Nehru followed by marrying a Zoroastrian and becoming Indira Gandhi. But these marriages were still exceptional. In the India of today, inter-communal, inter-caste and inter-class marriages are so common that they excite no comment nor any interest; they are just taken for granted. Needless to say, in all these marriages there was and is no question of either party changing his or her religion.

The ICS had a *biradari* of its own which included also members of the other Imperial Services. Once again there was no question of anybody being ever remotely concerned with the others' religion. There was a clear-cut line of demarcation between the British officers and the Indians, but between the Indians themselves there was no question of a division on the basis of one's beliefs. The Punjab, to which province I was allotted, was a Muslim-majority Province. Given also my own background of greater acquaintance with Islamic than with Hindu culture, it was only natural that the intimate friends I made were all Muslim. There were three friends I made during my service in the Punjab with whom my relations were those of a member of the family. They were Aminuddin of the ICS, who ended his career as Governor of Sindh, Qurban Ali Khan of the Indian Police, who became Governor of Punjab, and Mueenuddin of the ICS, a scion of another noble family with whom my maternal ancestors had been on terms of intimacy. I was younger than these three; I was treated as a younger brother and there was an extraordinary sense of protection which they felt towards me. Whenever I had a problem, it was to them that I quite naturally turned; it was they who gave me guidance. It was Saida, Amin's wife, to whom we entrusted the care of our infant son whenever we went out of station—not to that of any of our Hindu friends.

When I entered the Government of India, the ICS *biradari* was wider and more varied. But it again so happened that among the new friends I made or the old friends with whom my ties were strengthened, a wholly disproportionate number were also Muslims. To name but a few, some of whom rose to high positions in Pakistan, Ghulam Ahmed of the Indian Police, Ikramullah of the ICS, and Nawabzada Liaquat Ali at whose house in Delhi, now the Pakistani High Commission, we spent many a delightful evening, playing tennis and bridge. Old friendships also expanded—with Ghulam Mohammed (the same who became President of Pakistan), somewhat older than us but very young at heart, and 'Din' Tyabji and Azim Hussain, both Punjabi civilians like myself.

It was not that I deliberately chose Muslim friends; far from it. I had many friends of other religions, Hindu, Sikh, and Christian. The closeness of the bond between us was that of the *mushtarika tahzeeb* in which religion was irrelevant. None of the Muslim friends I have named, except Qurban, were overtly religious. Many of them ate forbidden meat and some of them drank forbidden liquor. The bond was one of language, of values, of attitudes towards life, of family background and class. Religion is certainly one of the factors which unites social groups, but to think that it is the only uniting factor is as mistaken as Karl Marx's belief that class alone is the bond that unites human beings.

The winds of change overtook the comfortable, leisurely, carefree, peaceful life that the upper class lived till only a few years before Independence and Partition. It had become increasingly clear over the years that no matter how much they might resent it, the British would some day or the other have to permit the Indians to take charge of their own destiny. Nobody in India was really aware that by the 1930s the will to power which was embodied in the doctrine of imperialism had already disappeared in Britain. Nor could anybody foresee that Hitler would so weaken the colonial powers that after the War they would simply not have the strength to retain their unwilling colonies. The total disappearance of Britain from the Indian scene as early as 1947 was therefore unexpectedly premature.

Under the absoluteness of British colonial rule, the religion of a member of the subject race did not matter. But any indication that there might some day be given to this subject race the power to manage its own affairs immediately raised the question of what would be the share of the religious communities in such power, no matter how minute or theoretical it might be, as they were to be vested with. The Hindus, who had taken to English education much earlier than the Muslims, did not really bother about this because, I suppose, it never occurred to them that anybody but they, because of their majority in the population, reinforced by their advanced education, would get the major share in it. The Muslims, not having kept pace with the times, found themselves a backward community. They felt that unless they asserted their separate identity, the great Hindu majority would swallow them up.

The building up of a separate Muslim political identity started with the efforts of Sir Syed Ahmed Khan to modernize his co-religionists. The debates between him and Badruddin Tyabji at the turn of the century showed clearly the two paths open to the Muslims. One was to separate religion from politics and, while keeping one's own religious identity, to merge in political terms with the larger Indian national community. The other was to convert the religious community into a separate political one. Sir Syed won his case with the majority of the Muslims of India; the nationalist Muslims, as they were called, were far fewer in number.

The seeds of the Partition were laid by that decision. There had always been two opposite tendencies at work in

India. One was the movement towards the integration of the Muslims with the other religious communities among whom they lived; the other was for the separation of the Muslims from the followers of other religions and the building up of a separate Muslim 'nation'. The Muslim leadership, trained in Aligarh and dominated in its thinking by that of the static and reactionary *taluqdaari* thinking, lent its considerable weight to the second tendency. The consequence over a period of time was that, while the other religious communities—the Hindus, the Christians, the Sikhs, the Parsis, the Jains, the Buddhists—all had as their sole aim the freedom of India, the majority of the Muslim community was not as interested in freedom as in the safeguarding of its position in a free India. This was what led to the demand, naturally very eagerly granted by the British, for separate electorates and reservations; as time showed, there could have been no more divisive a device invented.

Having decided that the Muslims were a separate nation, it became necessary to de-emphasize all the bonds which united, such as the commonality of dress and language, and emphasize all the factors which separated. It was on the commonality of religion that the Muslim nation was to be founded. But the trouble was that Islam, like any other live religion, had developed into many sects. Some, like the Khojas (of whom the Quaid-i-Azam was the most eminent), Bohras, and Kutchi Memons in western India, having been converted *en masse,* had kept many of their Hindu customs and beliefs and their customary personal (Hindu) law. Like the Sufis (whose philosophies were almost identical with the Vedanta) in northern India, particularly Kashmir, they preferred to pray at their own places of worship rather than at the regular mosque. If religion was to be the basis of unity, it was necessary to return to fundamentalism—whence, among other things, the Shariat Act of 1937 came. This was, of course, an internal Muslim matter. If the Muslims wanted to turn their face backwards it was nobody else's concern but theirs.

But what did concern others—the vast number of non-Muslim Urdu speakers and Urdu lovers (such as myself)—was the incredible declaration that Urdu was the language of the Muslims of India. The leadership seems not to have known that the Muslims of India spoke whatever was the language of their region, like their neighbours, and did not, for the most part, understand one word of Urdu. In all the non-Hindi speaking areas, East, West and South India, no Muslim could understand Urdu any more than his neighbours of different religions. The assumption that Urdu, being the language of Indian Islam, should be spoken by all Muslims, led, along with other causes, to the tragedy of the break-up of Pakistan and the emergence of Bangladesh.

It had its comic side too. Pandit Motilal Nehru told me that in 1928 (when he was the President of the Indian National Congress) he was coming back to Allahabad from Calcutta by the Howrah Mail. He was sitting in his compartment near the open window when a gentleman in a frock coat and a *turki topi* (the wearing of which, incidentally, was a punishable offence in Turkey) came up to him and said, *'Aap hi Ponditji hae'*, to which Panditji replied that he was. The gentleman in the red cap was very effusive: *'Bauri khoshi hoa aap se milke, bauri khoshi hoa'*. Panditji said he could not help saying, *'Achchha aap bhi Urdu bolte hain'*. At which the gentleman, highly excited at the insulting implication replied, *'Hain, boley ga noin, boley ga noin, nobi Mian ka joban...!'*

'The rift in the lute' ultimately 'made the music mute'. The rift then created went on widening: the more separate the Muslims felt and insisted aggressively on demonstrating, the more did the Hindus react against them. The Indian National Congress attempted to live up to its name but was aware that, though it had substantial support among the Muslims in the North-West Frontier and in Sindh, it had the support of only a minority of the Muslims of the UP and Bihar where their leadership lay. Its attitude towards the Muslim League was throughout ambivalent; sometimes it accepted, even though by implication, the League's claim to the leadership of the Muslim community; at others it said it represented the Muslims also. Mahatma Gandhi, in a desperate attempt to bring the Muslims into the national fold, linked the Khilafat Movement with the Non-co-operation Movement of the 1920s. But when the Khilafat itself disappeared as a result of Kamal Ataturk himself abolishing it, so did the Muslim-majority support for Indian freedom. The twenties and thirties witnessed the growth in communal riots, the forties were a period of confrontation, and from 1945 onwards, when it was absolutely clear that Indian freedom was round the corner, this bitterness was at its height.

It was during these years that communal consciousness finally disrupted the *mushtarika tahzeeb* of which the elite was so proud and in which it felt so comfortable. The tragedy was that even in the *biradari* of the ICS and the Imperial Services, there came the shadow of communal consciousness. It became necessary at that time to display one's Islam as ostentatiously and aggressively as possible. Even many of my closest Muslim friends stopped drinking alcohol, at least in public, and ostentatiously refused to touch pig meat. Some of them even started attending to their prayers.

But the female, as is well-known, is deadlier than the male; the most aggressive were the women. The first change came in their dress. The sleeves of the blouse which normally ended at the elbow now started ending below the wrist. The second change came when it was decided that the sari, which was their normal dress till then, was Hindu and should be given up in favour of the *shalwar kameez*. But later it was decided that even this dress was not Islamic enough because it was the common dress of all the women of north-western India; Hindu and Sikh women wore it quite as much as the Muslims. So then finally came the *gharara,* imported from the court of Wajid Ali Shah and certified to be truly Islamic by no less a person than Begum Liaquat Ali Khan herself. Fortunately, it did not catch on; its wearers, even until Partition, were limited; afterwards it was, of course, unnecessary.

But the most irritating and provocative behaviour was that when these ladies went to dinner to non-Muslim houses, they would ask ostentatiously whether the meat served was *jhatka* or *halal.* My wife's standard answer was 'I haven't the foggiest idea', at which the meat was left untouched though both guests and hosts knew well that it came from the same butcher as their own!

My very dear friend, then and now, Sughra Ikramullah, was the wildest among the protagonists of Pakistan. The enthusiasm of youth caused her genuinely to believe that there could never be any understanding between the Hindu and the Muslim. Once the Hindus were got rid of, Pakistan was established, and only the *pak* remained, it would be pure heaven. I have a feeling that she thinks somewhat differently now! But one incident in her crusade for her cause I remember well and must relate. I had made fun of this *halal and jhatka* syndrome, at which Sughra was angry. She explained heatedly that it was absolutely essential that every Muslim must eat nothing but *halal* meat. Why should I object to the Muslims following their religion? This was a typical Hindu attitude of mind. Would I, for instance, eat beef? I think she was quite flabbergasted at my answer that I would with pleasure. She thought I was merely boasting and challenged me to come and have beef with her at a picnic lunch next Sunday. This I did and gorged myself on well-spiced *muttar keema*—the spices disguising the extremely poor quality of Indian beef. Poor Sughra was rather nonplussed at finding somebody who took very lightly what he considered the idiocies of religion.

This kind of aggressive behaviour unfortunately left no pleasure in social life which, for this as for other reasons, gradually diminished. There were no more tennis and bridge-playing parties at Liaquat Ali's house, though this was really more because both he and his wife, Rana, had by then become great political leaders and had no time for social fripperies. But the bonds of life-long friendships cannot be easily snapped. There was a hiccup in some relationships but they were soon restored and fully mended. One took off, when one went to Pakistan, from the point at which one had earlier been; the intervening tensions were forgotten. I used to go to Karachi on official work fairly often. Whenever I did I stayed with Aminuddin; there was no dearth of hospitality in his house!

The fact is that there could have been no two men more secular than the Quaid-i-Azam or his Prime Minister, Nawabzada Liaquat Ali Khan, although I dare say no Muslim of such high education as Mr Jinnah could really be uninterested in the religion into which he was born. He was in essence an Englishman, as was his counterpart in India, Jawaharlal Nehru. Religious intolerance was to them anathema. But politics forced Mr Jinnah into raising a religious monster which he found, as often happens, he could not later control.

India and Pakistan are now two separate countries. Their people are developing in different ways. The *mushtarika tahzeeb* is dead. Most of those who are alive today did not know it and therefore do not miss it. But the remnants of a bygone age cannot help mourning the demise of an era of tranquility, leisure, grace, and elegance, and the sweet fragrance that still lingers of the *mushtarika tahzeeb*.

Shehla Shibli

Shehla Shibli, a creative writer from a prominent pre-partition family of the Punjab, has come to be known for the humorous twist in her writing. She has been associated with the English daily *Dawn* almost since its inception.

Known under the name Sheila Samir before partition, she worked at the All-India Radio (AIR) and was based in Lahore, Lucknow, and New Delhi. After her marriage she settled down in Lahore and joined the C&MG *(Civil and Military Gazette)* in 1946, where she started a women's page. In 1947, she went over to the new daily, *The Pakistan Times,* at the bidding of Faiz Ahmed Faiz, and started a page for women there also.

Since 1949, she has been in Karachi, first engaged in teaching English in colleges like the Government College for Women, and the College of Home Economics, and then, after having switched over to journalism entirely, as the editor of the fortnightly journal *She.* She has been a freelance journalist, contributing syndicated articles, as well as writing for local magazines and the newspaper *Dawn.*

She has also written poems and essays in Hindi, Urdu and English and these have appeared in both Indian and Pakistani publications. Her short stories have appeared in collections like *Mera Pasandeeda Afsana* and *Naye Zaviaye,* and she has contributed to anthologies of original nursery rhymes.

Either, Neither, or Both

Shehla Shibli

It was early in 1946 that I decided to get married—to Shibli, a Muslim. By then he had contributed seven succulent *raans* (legs of sacrificial animals) to the household over seven Eid-ul-Azhas and I was impressed. My family, who had partaken of the same *raans* and enjoyed eating them, remained unimpressed to the extent of disapproval. They said the times were also wrong for inter-communal marriages, which could overnight become international and cause problems. Friends, they told me, had been known recently to turn into enemies in some cases. Etc., etc.

But since they saw that the taste of the *raans* lingered on my lips, Father declared all our property as refugee property, including our Model Town bungalow which he had originally put in my name. In this he had listened to the advice of his next-door neighbour and friend, Sardar Nihal Singh, who had told him that my life would be made unsafe by Muslim predators, who would think nothing of plunging a knife in my chest to acquire the property. My father shuddered, looked into Shibli's innocent eyes, and wavered. But he was in strong hands, which held bridge cards evening after evening when four friends sat together to dissect the political situation changing around them. He succumbed and soon after left Lahore to join my brother in Delhi, where he had set up his medical practice. He had chosen Delhi because Father had too many friends in Lahore, all entitled to free medicines as well as advice.

Why Father left is another story. With the turn of the tide, all his personal staff of servants, Muslim as well as Hindus, had left. The huge bungalow remained unswept, while garbage piled inside as well as outside on the road. Lawns were littered with fallen leaves, broken twigs, and the eleven *seers* of milk which our pedigree cow delivered daily remained curdling in the pots and pans, till we were falling short of utensils to hold them, for our *gawala* was the only worker who continued his daily visits to milk the cow, to our extreme discomfort. After Pakistan was declared, my husband and I gave the cow to him as a present, because there was no grass left in the fields to feed her. The cow, when he pulled her ropes to draw her away from the house, refused to budge. But when at last she felt she had no recourse, kept turning and looking back at us in sorrow, and there were tears in her eyes.

Nor was the accumulating milk the only serious problem Father had to encounter. My infant son's napkins had grown into a menace with his running tummy. There was no way to fight this, as my Ayah had deserted us. Then there was an accumulating number of milk bottles facing Father, a heart patient. When my sister-in-law blamed him for his heartless partiality in choosing me against her and my brother, and remaining in Lahore for my sake, he gave way, and left.

Brought up in the wilds of Kashmir in a progressive family of Hindus, we had remained totally unfamiliar with problems of race, creed, or colour. Our coterie of friends had always included boys and girls of every kind and community. Our servants were selected with the same sentiment. My very first Ayah in Jammu had been Mehro, or Mehr Bibi, and the second in Kashmir was Janan—again a Muslim.

If we found a difference in the mode of living, praying or eating of our friends and staff, neither we nor our parents felt alienated, since the same God, we were told, had created us all. He had delighted in creating a vast variety of people in the Universe and so should we delight in it. We did.

The main divisive difference that made the orthodox hostile was that Muslims were meat-eaters, including the flesh of beef. The orthodox among Hindus were vegetarians, and spurned this practice of killing animals, specially resenting the killing of the cow who yielded milk. This made them exclude Muslims from their kitchens even when they befriended them. We, a family of meat-eaters, had no such problem with our friends, and shared our meals with them happily.

There were other divisive practices which were created by forces alien to our way of thinking. It seemed funny to us that while all Hindu girls in schools were taught Hindi and English, Hindu boys learnt Urdu and English. That may have been one of the reasons for my early rejection of the primitive local school, considering my deep interest in Urdu poetry, and the Ghazals we went about singing in the house. The immediate cause, however, was when I saw the Head Mistress open out the hair of a young low-middle-class girl, and comb it before the whole class into a tight plait. This kind of indignity, even though there was not the remotest chance of it coming my way (my father being a member of the Board of Trustees, for one thing) could not be tolerated. No amount of persuasion would make me enter the premises of the school again. A bright Kashmiri teacher was engaged to coach me at home. His name was Shri Dhar Joo Kachru and he took me right up to Matric level. My brothers' Urdu teacher was Master Hukam Singh, from whom I also took lessons.

By the end of September, the tourist season in the beautiful valley would officially be over, and visitors would have left for their homes. So would the sons and daughters of officers studying in colleges in the plains. We would then find ourselves shut in the valley with only a few families, and consequently grew close to them. There were the families of Ministers in the Kashmir government to meet, and doctors, businessmen, and politicians, and palace parties for our parents to attend. We made friends with their children, played and shared confidences irrespective of their religion. For there were several Ministers who were Muslims. There was Nawab Khusro Jang, Maulvi Nazir Ahmad, Abdul Qayyum, etc. The doctors similarly were from different religions, among whom I remember there being a Dr Abdul Wahid whom my mother always referred to as Abdul Wahid who had a large family. There was a doctor named Abdullah, whose daughter Naima became our friend, and specially so after she joined Kinnaird College in Lahore, and I followed her there later.

What I noticed, even as a teenager, was that while girls from Muslim families were all our friends, the boys were kept apart, and though we saw them moving about and sometimes salaaming us, they didn't join our play groups, the only exception being Ejaz, the son of Minister Qayyum, who would visit us with or without his extremely beautiful mother Mahmuda, who was friends with my mother. Always a loner, Ejaz seemed to take his mother's early death very hard.

We lost sight of him for years, until I came across a news item in a local daily some years ago. Ejaz had committed suicide in London. We were all horrified and saddened.

Among our particular friends were Balraj Sahni, his brother Bhisham, and their several cousins, and when I say several, I really mean just that, for there were hordes of them. Balraj later came to be known as a film actor and a writer, having secured awards for both. Bhisham, now a great writer in both Hindi and English, was my classmate in Government College Lahore later. Though Balraj is no more, the rest of us who are still up and about remain 'thick as thieves', and meet in Bombay and Delhi almost every year. In our fold now are also his nephews and nieces and their children and grandchildren.

India's Independence Movement, which had been triggered after the First World War when the British rulers had made promises of bestowing partial self-rule on us in return for utilizing all kinds of our resources, in men and material, and then failed us, had gained momentum when the Jallianwala murders took place in Amritsar, in which all who attended a meeting were hacked to pieces by orders of Generals Dyer and O'Dwyer. Now, years later, the freedom movement was at its peak, with Mahatma Gandhi's launching of his 'non-violent non-co-operation' protest against foreign occupation of the subcontinent, and the resultant high-handedness of the rulers imposed on the country. We were directed to boycott all foreign imports, discard the foreign clothing which only fed their Lancashire mills, and impoverished India. Instead, we were asked to promote our cottage industry, take to hand-spinning as a symbol of our declaration of independence. The spinning-wheel movement sprang up overnight, and wearing home-spun clothing was taken to by all freedom lovers, Hindu, Muslim, Christian and Parsi alike, with enthusiasm. I refer to the Raja of Mahmudabad's statement made after the Jallianwala massacre: 'The interest of the country is paramount, whether we are Muslim or Hindu...'

We were united against a powerful foreign enemy. The All-India Congress was the common platform for all, and included people like Mr M. A. Jinnah, Maulana Azad, Hakim Ajmal and Dr M. A. Ansari, who held the presidentship of Congress at one time.

Though removed from the mainstream of action in the far-away, rarefied atmosphere of the Kashmir valley, the intense movement had managed to seep in to every home, till all of us in schools, colleges and at home were wearing *khadi,* cumbersome and heavy as it was, and feeling proud of being a part of the great movement. Some of the boys of our acquaintance even became active revolutionaries, and plunged right into the heart of the movement.

I remember one of our friends, a young boy named Prem Dutt (not to be confused with the great revolutionary Bhagat Singh's friend Dutt), who joined the same group, and gained instant fame by throwing a shoe at a magistrate in a Lahore court where the Bhagat Singh Conspiracy Case was under trial. He was confined to prison for years, where he turned himself into a linguist and scholar, with a long beard. He certainly made good use of his detention.

While many of the freedom fighters had returned their titles and their *jagirs* bestowed on them by the British rulers, my sole contribution to the non-violent movement was, perhaps, only in sticking to *khadi* apparel, and applauding the sacrifices of others.

Later, in 1920, tables started to be turned when the Arya Samaj leader Swami Daya Nand started his *shuddi* movement with the mass conversion of some lower-class Muslims. This horrible move by one fanatic rightly angered and alienated the Muslims, until the newly-formed Muslim League broke up. Disgusted with the way things were turning, Jinnah took himself off to England, and remained there till 1937. On his return, he suggested the formation of a Muslim League-Congress Coalition, but failed to settle the terms. This was the first signal of the parting of the ways to come.

Those of us who were not old enough to absorb the implications of the political currents working in our midst remained untouched. Brought up in the lush valley with dancing rivulets and prancing horses, those friends with whom we shared this experience will ever remain close to our hearts. We will remember the shared deep silences of winter, the haunting melodies like *Goshe matija na no* ringing through the hills, or hummed by a lovely paddy grinder—that vision of a celestial being—a young girl dressed in rags in a stance which would put a queen to shame.

Qudrat-Ullah Shahab was also roaming about in the same sphere, his brother being a doctor in the State Hospital. He was a friend of my brother. Lately, wading through my books, I found two, *Silas Marner* and *Scenes of Clerical Life* by George Eliot, with the inscription, 'Presented by a friend to J.C.B. as a humble token of love for his literary intellect', signed Qudrat-Ullah Shahab, dated 15 July 1936.

Our family entered the valley in 1926 when my father was posted in the Civil Hospital there on his return from Edinburgh, where he had gone for his F.R.C.S. I remember the first evening we walked into the house allotted to us. It was on the outskirts of the hospital in Srinagar in Mira Kadal area on the banks of the River Jhelum. My elder sister opened the windows of our bedroom, and there was the River Jhelum with *shikaras* (boats) plying on it, and the *manjies* (boatmen) singing lustily. There were only a few house-boats, mostly vacant, it being the month of November when visitors had long departed for warmer climes. The trees had shed their leaves, and stood in their bare majesty on the other side of the bank, while Mount Shankracharya, now known as *Takht-i-Sulaiman,* loomed in the distance, looking remote and yet approachable. We were awed, and fell under its spell. Friendships that we formed in such surroundings could not be torn from our hearts, nor the nostalgia wished away easily. It has become a part of us.

Sometimes, accompanying father on his nightly hospital rounds, I would see many Muslim women with their stomachs burnt. This kind of accident was common there, and was caused by *kangries* which the poor carried hidden under their gowns. A *kangri* is a kind of cane basket fitted with an earthern pot for holding coal covered with ash to provide warmth.

I asked my father how these people could be poor when the gorgeous valley they lived in was fragrant with rich saffron fields ripening under the sun, and factories around producing costly *pashmina* and lovely silks. How could any one lack for food either, when the trees were dripping with ripe cherries and peaches, and there in the fields grew luscious strawberries waiting to be picked. All this was theirs, wasn't it? They were the original inhabitants of the valley, weren't they? So why...?

My father sighed, as if under great pressure. 'I know what you mean. All this is theirs, and yet not theirs. You will understand when you grow up.'

'But do *you* understand?' I asked, puzzled.

'Probably not, or only partially. It is painful to see so much poverty,' he said, sighing.

'I don't want to wait till I grow up to know, and that also only partially. I want to know it all now, this minute,' and I burst out crying, because that day I had seen our driver Ghulam Mohammad, son of our Ayah Janan, carry his little sister into the hospital. Her tummy had third degree burns on it. Noori was a beautiful child of seven who would sometimes come to the house with Janan and play with me. I had taken her to heart, and so had my parents.

What would I learn when I grew up? As it happened, quite a lot, and that was mostly about my own helplessness to do anything for the people of the valley I loved so single-mindedly.

Visitors to Kashmir came from all corners of the world, and included unknown figures from the world of art and literature with whom we were to grow closer and closer as we grew. Among them were people like the famous poet of the continent Faiz Ahmad Faiz, Sufi Ghulam Mustafa Tabassum, Rashid Ahmad (later Director-General Broadcasting, Pakistan), artists like Ahmad Saeed Nagi, and S. N. Sanyal who was later to marry a first cousin of ours. Dr Taseer came, and worked in the valley as Principal of the Sri Partap College after we had left.

And one day a visitor announced was Swami Daya Nand, about whose *shuddi* and *sangathan* programme we had heard of with extreme distaste. A fanatic amongst Arya Samajies, he had single-handedly been responsible for creating friction between the two major communities of India, Hindu and Muslim, and my father refused to have anything to do with him, to our delight. If I were to say that every Hindu of the times we knew felt the same way as my father did, perhaps I would not be correct. But if they felt any different, we younger members of the family had no means of knowing. It didn't, however, stop us from wondering why some Arya Samaji friends considered him worth entertaining.

Among my father's associates was the rebel Sheikh Abdullah, later known as the *Sher-i-Kashmir,* who was trying to wrest the rights of Muslims from the Hindu Raja Hari Singh. I remember his wife, the daughter of Kashmir's famous hotelier Nedou, who became a staunch Muslim. Her favourite song was:

Muskurate ja rahe ho, dil ko tarpane ke bad.
Bijlian chamka rahe ho, phul barsane ke bad

There she would sit, confident of her expertise, surrounded by smiling faces while she ran her slender fingers over the keys of a harmonium. I refused to smile, because she had told my sister (with a wink) that I shouldn't be allowed to wear rouge at such a tender age. To disprove this unfair charge, I had washed and washed my face until it got redder and redder. No, I didn't smile. Instead I laughed and laughed at her accent.

We got to know many Kashmiri families. There was Bakshi Ghulam Mohammad and his brother Majid, fond of clowning; there was Ghulam Sadiq. All these people, including Sheikh Abdullah, were dealers in *pashmina,* silks and carpets, and owned huge factories. They would hold rallies and demonstrations against the Dogra ruler of the state and his partisan policies. As the Chief Medical Officer of the state automatically became ex-officio superintendent of jails, Father in this capacity got to know and became very fond of these daredevils. If they smuggled cigarettes or notes in prison, Father would turn a blind eye to them.

Once he was summoned to the palace and charged with over-friendliness with Christians and Mussalmans. The Maharaja, who was fond of him, said to him, 'I hear you have a soft corner for them, and frequently share their meals also. As such, we refuse to have you at our table, or shake hands with you. You have become one of the untouchables for us.'

Father smiled, and said, 'Your Highness is right. I not only eat with them, but receive their vomit and their urine on my body when they are ill. But what worries me is that you, Your Highness, have been eating your meals with this untouchable of the lowest kind, and even embracing him. I think by now you are equally contaminated. I am afraid nothing can purify you now. Please discuss with Swami Daya Nand how to get purified. He has a huge *shuddhi* programme. Maybe he can make you a Hindu again.'

Luckily, the Raja saw the humour of the situation, and again folded him in his embrace. Since he was already contaminated, I suppose he thought one more time wouldn't matter.

In 1937 we had to leave Kashmir because of Father's health problems, and settled down in Lahore's Nisbet Road, near our grandparents. As by now we were all of us studying in Lahore, and going home to Srinagar only for our vacations in summer, we soon adapted ourselves to changed conditions. When our Model Town bungalow was built and ready to receive us, we shifted there in 1938.

Next year came World War II.

I was in Dalhousie convalescing after an attack of typhoid. I was also trying at the same time to work out a solution to a scrape I had got myself into through a disastrous marriage.

'We are at war,' I heard King George VI's voice announce. I looked at my counterpart in the episode of disaster and declared another war, on the personal front.

On returning to Lahore I joined All-India Radio as a reader and selector of material for broadcasting. A few months later I went through an interview to get into the regular cadre of AIR was selected and posted to Lahore where I shared an office with Hafiz Hoshiarpuri the poet, and Agha Bashir Ahmad, who ended his career in Pakistan as Director of Pakistan Television in Lahore.

I found a flutter of activity at the station. War was on, and though not India's war, strictly speaking, our soldiers were fighting on all fronts. Every radio programme we put forward was geared to the raging war. There were messages to be sent overseas, and received, entertainment programmes to be planned and projected. No matter what programme portfolio we held, all of us had our hands into everything. Anyone could find himself (or herself) suddenly called upon to become an announcer, a newsreader, a writer, an interviewer or a producer at an instant's notice. The next moment the same person would be required to fulfil the duties of a public relations officer to important speakers or world famous personalities, scientists or historians, people like Professor Toynbee, writers like E. M. Forster, artistes like Ustad Bare Ghulam Ali Khan, or dancers like Uday Shanker or Ram Gopal—in fact the works.

We would scour the town to hunt for talent, from drawing rooms and clubs, from village *mailas,* and from the red-light area of Lahore, *Hira Mandi* (diamond market). We would pull out speakers from government offices, from women's associations, and children from their schools. An alert eye had to be kept out for spotting important visiting celebrities. The cars at our disposal would forever be on the roads, despite strict petrol rationing, even for buying presents and chocolates for performing children. On days of late evening transmission duty, I would take a servant along and grope my way through streets, pitch dark because of blackouts. All hours were working hours for us as broadcasting was an essential service. The more demanding the work, the closer we all drew, irrespective of our caste, creed, social status, or communities. We were knit in a camaraderie of a common heritage. All broadcasters became ours, whether they were visiting artistes or local ones, from Gangu Bai Hangal, Timir Baran or Begum Akhter to classical dancers Uday Shanker and Ram Gopal, from poets Akhter Shirani, Josh Malihabadi. Faiz Ahmad

Faiz, Miraji and editors of newspapers and magazines. The station had recruited the most talented of the country's intelligentsia to its staff, which included writers like Krishen Chander, Mahmud Nizami, Rajinder Singh Bedi, in fact the top talent of the country. Petty problems which divided communities never had a chance with us. The dramatists we worked in close communication with were no less than Rafi Peer and Imtiaz Ali Taj.

The families we grew close to comprised almost the whole of Lahore—the Manzur Qadirs, the Fazal-i-Hussains, Justice M. H. Rehman and his brother Rahim. There were many Christian families, the Sondhies, the Chatterjies, the Singhas, the Bhanots, the Ram Chandras etc., who were prominent educationists and our friends. We had a vast coterie of Hindu and Sikh friends also. There was N. Iqbal Singh, and K. S. Duggal, writers and colleagues. N. Iqbal Singh, the writer of *Andaman Islands,* was for some reason referred to as 'Ikki, my love', and is still called that. Duggal, several of whose books lie on my shelves, married a girl from a top Muslim family who is a doctor. There was the volatile and prolific writer Khushwant Singh, and his handsome wife Kanwal, great friends of my sister and brother-in-law Som, and bosom friend of Manzur Qadir, and his wife my dear friend Asghari. In 1979, when I was a guest in her daughter's house in Washington, D.C., along with my son, Asghari regaled him with stories of my college days, such as when cycling with my brother on Davis Road, we were laughing so much that we both fell off our cycles.

Life on the personal level soon ceased to be a bed of roses for me, in the wake of a couple of heart-rending deaths in 1942, so I made up my mind to go away from Lahore, and opted for Lucknow. I found it just the place for shedding off my blues, and was utterly enchanted with its aristocratic charm and old-world hospitality.

The music that emanated from Lucknow Studios was nothing short of pure inspiration. And no wonder. The artists at the disposal of the station were some of the topmost musicians of the era, people the subcontinent would boast of for ages to come. They were Ustad Alla-ud-din Khan of Mahiar, *sarod nawaz;* Ustad Sundu Khan, *sarangi nawaz;* Ustad Fayyaz Khan, vocalist; the young upcoming Ustad Ali Akbar Khan, *sarod nawaz,* the son of the maestro Alla-ud-din Khan, with magic in his fingers. Surely he was on his way to vie with, and perhaps outshine his illustrious father Ravi Shanker, the *sitar* maestro. There was Rasoolan Bai with her melodious *thumries,* Akhter Begum the enchanting singer with her sparkling *dadras* and *chaities,* and many others.

Many a morning I would wake up in the early hours and go to Ali Akbar's house to hear him practise in the next room, while I would sip tea with his wife, drowning myself in the music. On other mornings Akhter Begum would breeze in, put me in her car, and take me home with her. Akhter was married to a tall handsome barrister from a *taluqdar* family, Ishtiaq Hussain. 'I am keeping a tiger in my den,' Ishtiaq Bhai would say, referring to Akhter's volatile artistic temperament.

At the studios, Rasoolan Bai would draw me into the music studio, and sing to me her latest *thumri.*

No, I was not in charge of the music section. I was put in the Features Section, where I was in close touch with the humourist Shaukat Thanvi. Shaukat Bhai was a dynamic writer, scribbling away while he talked, turning out four or five copies of his features, handing them to the seasoned actors in our live studio, while I sat on the control panel, manipulating the switches with trembling fingers. No rehearsal was possible. But our artistes coped, though I still shudder when I recall the nervous tension this caused.

The atmosphere at the office was friendly and relaxed, and conducive to creative activity. The window of my office looked out at a magnificent garden area, with a huge leafy tree with over-hanging branches. During *barsat,* it would gather into itself the darkness of the looming clouds, and scoop up the showers in its foliage, reluctant to let them go. I would watch the whole scene with fascination, and thought of it as an embodiment of the grandeur of the spirit of Lucknow.

Our broadcasters included the topmost intellectuals of the age living in the UP among whom were the great poet Firaq who was specially partial to me. There was Niaz Fatehpuri, Sibte Hasan, and my friend Dr Rashid Jahan and her learned husband Dr Mahmud. Dr Rashid Jahan was the sister of Khursheed Mirza of PTV fame. We would look forward to having a bite with her often, specially when she treated us to *besani roti* with *bhindi bhujia*. My friend Maya Sirkar was there, living on Cowper Road. Later she married M. Jamil, came to live in Pakistan with him, and worked as Reader (and then also as Head of the English Department) in the Karachi University. Attiya Hussain, who was known as the number one beauty of Lucknow, (who later became Attiya Habibullah and worked for the BBC in London) lived in Lucknow and since her sister-in-law Asif Rishad (the youngest daughter of Sir Fazal-i-Hussain of Lahore) was a close friend of mine, I came to know Attiya well.

But alas, my days in Lucknow were numbered, and approaching their end, because of my servant Bakhtiar Ali. My old family servant Ram Singh, who had accompanied me from Lahore, had left, and I had substituted him with Bakhtiar Ali. A war veteran, Bakhtiar Ali had been discharged from the army because of shrapnel wounds, and had become my cook-bearer. He was asthmatic, and stingy. One day I got annoyed with him.

'I gave you a tenner a week ago. Why don't you spend it, and give me variety in my breakfast. If you don't spend money, I'll have to let you go.'

'*Dusehri* mangoes I bought yesterday were one rupee a *dhari* (consisting of thirty-three mangoes). Where should I spend the money!'

'Besides,' I continued cruelly, 'you cough and cough and put me off my food. How long can I put up with this? You'll have to go, I'm afraid.'

'Only my dead body will leave this house,' he announced, and picking up the tray, left.

Bakhtiar Ali died that day, crushed under a military jeep while crossing the road to buy eggs. Carrying a Neville Chamberlain umbrella on that rainy day, he met his end, while those of us on transmission duty waited for him to bring us our elevenses.

In the servants' quarters his wife with one son and a couple of hens did not know about the accident. Nor did we, until a news item next day reporting a stray death brought it to our notice. We verified the news, and brought his umbrella home for his forlorn wife.

With the police force of the town behind me, Akhter Begum's Barrister husband Ishtiaq Bhai as my counsel, and my journalist friend Jamal Kidwai as strong moral support, a campaign was lodged for getting adequate monetary reparation for the bereaved wife and son of Bakhtiar Ali. Since this necessitated my running around town at all hours of the day, I had to take days off from work. The Station Director, Jugal Kishore Mehra (who later married the Muslim artiste, Anwer Begum or Paroji, and lived in Pakistan as Ahmad Salman) and I had a serious difference over this, to resolve which, the Director General, Mr Ahmad Shah Bokhari, (Patras) came over to Lucknow himself. Though Jugal by this time had had second thoughts, I elected to go to Delhi with my old professor, and re-visited my beloved Lucknow only the next year (1944) to attend the wedding of my friend Maya with M. Jamil—still another intercommunal marriage. There seemed to be so many those days, the product of a common cultural integration over centuries of living together.

My friend Sadiqa (the sister of the film magnate W. Z. Ahmad who married an actress called Nina) had recently married a Hindu Barrister of Allahabad named Chander

Shekher. Satnam (Dr Satnam Charan Singh), another dear Sikh friend, had married Nawab Muzaffar Ali Khan's son Mahmud Ali Khan, and was living in Lahore with his family at the time. And all this on the personal front despite the deep clouds of dissent and disintegration gathering on the horizon. Then in 1945, Jamal Kidwai married a Sikh girl from a prominent family of the UP, Shakuntala Jaspal.

Coming to think of it all now, it seems ironic that so many of the intelligentsia should have been hunting for solutions other than those the politicians were engaged in finding. We all start life asking questions. But it seems the only ones who find clear cut answers are politicians—and computers, having been programmed that way.

The significant fact is that none of these marriages broke up, despite the various kinds of pressures they must have had to encounter during half a century of living together. Some record this, for the historian of the future to assimilate and ponder over. Nor did some others break up which took place within the next two years before 'the Great Divide' of 1947. These were of two of my All-India associates, Iqbal Malik, and Batra with whom I was to share an office on my arrival in Delhi. Iqbal was to marry a Hindu Bengali girl, Amita Roy, also a colleague and a friend. Amita and I also shared living accommodation allotted to us by AIR in Babar Lane, Delhi. Batra became a Muslim to marry Khurshid, and went over to the BBC in London, where he became an OBE as Shahid Latif.

Our announcer at Lucknow station, Aley Hasan, who also migrated to London and joined the BBC, married a girl-friend, Krishna. This marriage broke up under special circumstances—an addiction in Aley being the cause. But he never recovered from the pain of the parting, he told me when I saw him last in 1968 at the BBC Club in London.

Then there was Krishen Chander, the short-story writer who married Salma, daughter of another famous writer, Rashid Ahmad Siddiqi, and started a happy period of married life, and continued to live happily with her till his death, which in other words means ever after.

In the meantime, political events were moving towards a different course. On 23 March 1940 came the Pakistan Resolution, with the demand of autonomy for units of Muslim predominance. Areas like the North-West Provinces were to be grouped together to constitute independent states in which these units would be autonomous and sovereign. The Cripps Mission of 1942 recognized the concept, but nothing came of it, as the Cripps offer did not meet the requirements of the Muslim League.

In 1945 the World War ended, and in August 1946 the League launched a programme of Direct Action to achieve Pakistan. It met strong resistance among its opponents in all the provinces of the country. There were bloodbaths in Calcutta, Sylhet, Noakhali, and Tipperah, with forced conversion and abductions. Not all the efforts of the Muslim League and the Congress could stem the frightful image of hostility which loomed up to engulf the whole of the subcontinent. Many relationships built over the years fell prey to a new hatred and distrust, and a turmoil ensued.

I was in Lahore while all this was happening, and about to give birth to my baby. It was now the summer of 1947, and the date was 12 April when I had the first intimations to get to the hospital.

The hospital where I had been registered was the Aitchison, Lahore in the vicinity of Gwalmandi, where a friend of mine, Qamar Khan, was an R.M.O. The whole of Lahore was under curfew, and getting to the hospital was going to be a real problem. We required passes to get through the protected curfew area from Model Town, and did not have time to do so. I thus found myself being escorted to the hospital by my husband driving with a cigarette in his mouth and a double-barrelled gun by his side. Next to him sat his younger brother Saad Tarique (later a Major-General in the Pakistan Army) a bachelor, also with a gun and a cigarette, tense as tense could be. At the back sat the newly-married wife of our cook with me, inexperienced and hysterical. None of my escorts had any idea of what an exercise of this kind entailed. Thus we passed through a ghost-like Lahore, dark and sinister, smelling danger at every step. But no one stopped us, and thanking our stars we reached the hospital. My escorts, then ran to summon Dr Qamar Khan from her room. She was taking a shower, and shouted to them to find nurses to carry me to the labour room. My husband and Saad went to the labour room, but found it completely deserted. The whole staff had run to see a huge fire which was raging in the area near the hospital. They picked up a stretcher on their own and put me on it. I was put on a table with no one around except my own escorts, with the cook's wife screaming *'Hai Bibi ji'* and crying loudly. Then Qamar came running, with her long wet hair covering her from head to foot, and pushed the family out of the room just in time, and I sighed with relief. Within minutes the problem was over, and the swarming nurses and the head doctor were all recounting to me the stories of the fire around Gwalmandi in vivid details which I hardly heard, for a peaceful sleep was stealing on me.

By now Lahore was seething with political unrest and exploding in communal riots, mostly around the University area, hence they were termed 'the University riots'. The tension while the country waited for the announcement declaring Pakistan as an independent sovereign state was not only tangible but pulsating.

It was at this time that a wedding in my husband's family took us all to Delhi. It was early July, and my son was just over two months old. With me went a newly-employed ayah named Akhter, who within days married a Hindu Brahmin and left me without any remorse.

After the wedding of my sister-in-law Bilqees (who acquired a new name, Saba Zahir), on 12 July the rest of the family went back to Lahore, including my husband, while I stayed back with my father and elder sister. Bilqees stayed in Delhi because her husband Zahir Azar was on the Partition Committee along with M. Shoaib (later of the World Bank). She told me later that they had an armed guard of sixty to protect them, and to escort them two months later, up to Bombay.

On 14 August, Pakistan was duly declared an independent country, and the next day, British rule in India formally came to an end. India was at last free from the stranglehold of a foreign yoke after a long, long struggle. It was an occasion for great joy, but it was being spoilt by wide-spread reports of looting and carnage from both parts of the subcontinent. Nevertheless, frantic preparations went on in New Delhi, the capital of India, to make 15 August— India's day of Independence—an outstandingly festive occasion. No police were to be posted anywhere near the site of the celebrations, where an impressive rostrum was set up. Cars were parked for miles around the site, from where we had to walk to our seats. There on the rostrum stood a beaming Jawaharlal Nehru, the hero of the Independence Movement, now the new Prime Minister of the country, nodding and waving. Sitting around him were Sardar Patel and the other members of the Indian Congress hierarchy. There also sat Lord Mountbatten with his consort, the famous Lady Edwina. Everyone was smiling and seemed at ease. Speeches boomed on loudspeakers, while the audience laughed and clapped, clapped and laughed till all track of time seemed to be lost in the ensuing light-hearted banter and general friendliness. It certainly was a great day for the whole of the subcontinent to have been able to shake off the yoke which had long held the country in subjugation to a foreign power. But in the back of our minds was a painful reminder of something lacking in the Assembly. A large part of the stalwarts who had fought with the Indian Congress, and made sacrifices along with them for the freedom of the country, were missing. Suddenly a great cloud seemed to descend on me, till I was clutching my heart. Wildly I looked around, desperately trying to locate myself amongst all those carefree faces, and froze. Where in God's name was I? I shook myself with an effort, and stood up in a panic. I felt my sister's hand pull me to her lovingly till I was drawn to her lap with my head hidden in her neck. Horses seemed to be racing inside me, strumming against my chest relentlessly. Somebody had forsaken somebody somewhere. Who, how, and why? Politicians seemed to have all the answers. Had I any?

Soon it was time to make a move. We wandered round for the best part of an hour looking for our car, and at last stumbled upon it by chance. We drove home in complete silence, looking unseeingly at the architectural splendour abounding all around, vast verdant lawns spread everywhere, fountains, fields, monuments. On reaching home, we found our compound full of people, cousins, friends and acquaintances who had arrived from different parts of the country, and some from Pakistan, among whom was my younger brother. Our family being an amalgam of both Hindu and Muslim cultures, we were to receive news from both sides, all heart-rending, stupefying, earth-shaking.

Thenceforth, every day brought us blood-curdling stories. Trainloads of Muslims making for Pakistan were butchered, their women raped and inhuman indignities heaped on them. A prominent economist, Brij Narain, was murdered in Lahore. A prominent Muslim of India, Shafi Ahmad Kidwai, who had set up a refugee camp in New Delhi for the migrants, was butchered. Worried to distraction, we would try to book calls to Pakistan, but couldn't get through for the operators on both sides shouting 'Pakistan *murdabad*', or 'Jawaharlal Nehru *murdabad*'. Then would come a thud, cutting us off.

There was nothing for me to do except try and get to Pakistan. I was told there was a waiting list of 14,000 passengers with the airline, and the chances of getting to

Pakistan alive were slim. My brother-in-law Som Nath Chib who had opted for Pakistan (the first Asian recipient of a Hall of Fame) but had been made to retract, somehow managed to get me a seat on 3 September. All our friends and relations were appalled. They appealed to my father to stop me from going, threw their *pagries* and hats at my feet, but my father held them back. 'She has her commitment to fulfil. Let her go.'

The scene I met at the old Lahore airport at Walton Training Centre was, to say the least, grim. There was a police cordon to stop all passengers from leaving the airport. While I stood bewildered, holding my screaming infant in my arms, a young Pakistani came up to me and said, 'Mrs Shibli, I am Hadi, a pilot, and a friend of your husband. He asked me this morning to meet you and escort you home to Model Town. Please come with me.'

'My husband asked you? But he doesn't know, I mean how could he...?'

'I wouldn't know that,' and saying this he started loading my luggage in his car, put me in a seat next to him, and whisked me away.

Within minutes, I found myself deposited outside my brother-in-law Zubair's house in Model Town along with my luggage. I turned round to thank Hadi, but he seemed to have disappeared. Instead I was surrounded by my sister-in-law and her family.

'There she is. She has come. Didn't we all say she would, and wasn't he right when he said it would be today?' And I was pulled into warm embraces, fed almonds, made to drink cold milk shake, while the baby was taken away somewhere to be kissed and cuddled.

'You must be fagged out, with your baby yet an infant. Here, lie down and I will press your legs,' said my sister-in-law Ismet, pushing me into a comfortable bed, and resolutely taking hold of my legs, disregarding all my protests.

'He is a clever manipulator, I must say. The way he talked me into giving up our six foot *mali* Omer to work for him, because he said he needs someone to look after you.'

'Who?' I ventured to ask, still in a daze.

'Who, indeed! Who else, except your husband?'

'But he couldn't possibly know my programme. I never...'

'Oh, he knew all right, believe me. There he is. You can see for yourself.'

And sure enough, there he was, jumping over the hedge of the lawn to join us, grinning.

He took us both, the infant and me, to my father's bungalow nearby. And as I entered, I found the house different. There was no furniture, no carpets, no curtains, only a couple of beds, without any bedding material on them. 'What...' I started to ask, but my husband hushed me.

'The house has been robbed through and through. But they didn't harm your younger brother. When your cousins brought along a chartered plane to take him to Delhi, they even came to bid him a warm good-bye.'

I was staggered. 'Who are "they" you are talking about?'

'It is the villagers from the nearby village of Bhavra. They looted the house, taking away everything.'

I was under too much shock to ask anything further and started to stare at the devastated garden outside. No flowers on the bushes, no leaves on the trees. 'Relax,' said my partner in life.

Then I laughed through falling tears.

'Surely the trees haven't been robbed of their leaves by our Bhavra gangs?'

'No. That is the doing of the refugees who have come to Pakistan ailing. They saunter in from the Walton Training School refugee camp looking for lemons and other fruit, and stay to ravage the trees. They come daily, and I don't have the heart to stop them.'

'Of course,' I said, 'though why they should stay as you said, and pull off leaves from the trees is something I don't understand.'

'Remember, this bungalow is Hindu property, and they have been embittered. This is their way of finding vent for it. Please keep inside the house, and don't take a step outside. I am going to throw all your saris away. You must wear nothing but shalwar suits from now on. As it is, I am having some problems with a Pakistani Major. He has lost some of his relations in India due to the bloodbath there, and keeps hounding me, asking me to hand you over to him as soon as you enter Pakistan. He must have learnt of your arrival by now, and if I know him, he will be back tomorrow. I told him he would have to walk over my dead body to get to you. Don't worry unduly. I am working on him and am soon going to make him understand our position. In the meantime, keep out of the way, for God's sake.'

I looked at him mutely, and was worried on both our accounts. What had we let ourselves into, I wondered.

That same night, Sardar Nihal Singh's servant next door was found murdered, and my security in the house tightened, but there was no earthly way to stop the baby from howling or gurgling when he wanted to. The Major came and went, heard the precious sounds of a happy baby, and slowly but surely started changing towards the indulgent father. Then his visits stopped, and we breathed freely.

I started to work in the Walton refugee camp. There I discovered all the quilts and the blankets which were missing from the house, and many other articles like suitcases which the Bhavra thieves must have spared, unless they were generous donors to the camp.

A few days later, Allah Jawai, who was an area masseur, appeared in our house, and offered her services. Besides which, she told me she had a message for me. It turned out to be a historic message sent to me by the Bhavra village thieves who had looted our bungalow. This is what Allah Jawai told me:

'They say we are sorry we had to rob you. As far as your Hindu property is concerned, we have vowed to leave you not a scrap. But your life we will protect with our own, have no doubt about that. It is not only because you have chosen to live here with us in Pakistan, but also because you are the daughter of a father who saved many of our lives, giving us medicines and medical advice free. Our loyalty is at your command.'

My God. What a country! What a people! My own now. Sentiments and loyalties, it seems, have a longer life than we give them credit for. With blood-bonds on both sides of the Divide, it is not easy for us to divide ourselves emotionally.

I must tell you of an old woman from Pakistan who recently travelled with me to Delhi.

'I wonder what the old city looks like now,' she mused. 'I am not even sure I will be able to recognize the *mohalla* where we used to live. They say everything is changed.'

'Then this must be the first time you are visiting India since Partition?'

'Yes, it is, and my thanks are due to our neighbours the Murari Lals who sent me a ticket to visit Delhi.'

'How have you kept in touch with them for so long?' I asked.

'The family has been visiting Pakistan frequently. During their last visit here, they asked me why I never visited India. They said they had arranged my visa, and would be sending me a ticket soon. This is the result, and I am now able to visit them in Delhi. I have an old sister there whom I never expected to see, but for this gesture of my old friends and neighbours.' I saw the old woman wiping her eyes.

No, it hasn't been easy for blood relations to be on different sides of the Divide, and be called upon to divide themselves emotionally. Perhaps it will, at some point, occur to the enlightened elements of both sides that this very emotion can be used to form the basis of a harmonious relationship. Until then we will have to stay positioned as we are and remain 'Either, Neither, or Both'.

Pandu Chintamani

Pandu Chintamani was born in 1934. Educated at St Columbia's High School and St Stephen's College, he obtained a degree in Economics and History (1954). He held senior management positions in ITC Ltd., EMI Plc., Rallies India Ltd., and was Director, Hindustan Thompson Associates Ltd. from 1992 until his death in 1996. He was the Chairman of Sportrak, and President of Think Tank 2001. He was also on the Visiting Faculty of the Management Development Institute, the Indian Institute of Mass Communication, and Jamia Millia Islamia. His literary activities included scripting and producing radio as well as television programmes and audio-visual presentations. He wrote several papers on Economic Strategy and stories of human interest. His wife Usha lives with their two daughters and a son in New Delhi.

The Hindu Son

Pandu Chintamani

It was early morning on a Sunday. The silence was broken by the ringing of the doorbell. My wife went to open the door while I was trying to snatch a few more minutes of sleep. I was rudely awakened by her announcement that Choki and Mangu, the part-time maids, had come to do the housework. When I asked why they had come so early on a Sunday, I was told that they wanted to leave early so that they could see the TV serial, *Ramayana* (the legend of the Hindu God-King). I was expounding on the piety of the poor when my wife reminded me that Choki and Mangu were in fact very pious Muslims. I was intrigued. I asked Choki how she, a Muslim, was interested in a Hindu legend. Choki replied, 'Sahib, our home town is Ayodhya. It doesn't matter whether Ram was a Hindu or Muslim. What matters is that he was our townsman.'

* * *

My memory went back to the September of 1941, when I was eating sandwiches and chocolate cake at the birthday party of my best friend, Inam Ikramullah. As a mutton sandwich was about to enter my mouth, a gentle hand stopped me. It was Inam's mother, Begum Shaista Ikramullah (Aunty Soghra to me). 'Do you think you should be eating mutton? Are you not a Hindu Brahmin? Your parents may accuse us of making you lose your caste'. I replied that as my mother and several of my siblings had succumbed to tuberculosis, my father encouraged me to eat non-vegetarian food. In my childish exuberance I went on to tell her that although my ancestors had been high caste Brahmins and trustees of the Kanchipuram temple complex, the first book my father had given me was the Holy Bible (the best 'English Reader', he said), and I even knew the first Kalma of the Koran.

During the next six years I became an adoptive member of the Ikramullah family. My father died and Inam's parents became mine—at least during weekends. Millions were dying on the battlefields of Europe and Asia; thousands died in the Hindu-Muslim riots in various parts of India. But to Inam and me, it was sandwiches and cakes and pulling the pig-tails of Salma and Naz. It did not matter that he was a Muslim and I a Hindu. What mattered was our companionship and the warmth of the Ikramullah home.

* * *

15 August 1947. As the Indian tricolour unfurled, I led the class choir in singing the National Anthem. I received a commemorative medal and a plaque. I hired a bicycle from Wahid, the owner of the cycle shop below our stairs (two annas an hour for normal makes; four annas an hour for the brand new green Raleigh). I rushed to show my trophies to Inam and the family. The house was in darkness. An international boundary had separated my adoptive family from me.

* * *

The euphoria of Independence was overshadowed by the holocaust that followed. Fires burnt all around Connaught Place, where we lived. Shops and homes were destroyed. Bodies lay rotting on the streets and pavements. I was afraid.

Suddenly I heard a roar on the street. My trembling legs took me to the balcony. A furious mob was chasing a frail figure. He disappeared under the colonade below. A couple of minutes later there was a frantic knock on the door. I was petrified. But a voice that I did not recognize as my own shouted, 'Who is it?' In a whispered gasp came the reply, 'Baba, this is Wahid. Please save my life.'

An unknown force helped me to open the latch and Wahid tumbled through the door. Even as I shot the bolt, a mob was hammering on the door threatening dire consequences if I did not hand him over. Wahid ran and locked himself in the toilet. I ran to the balcony and tried to climb to the roof. A burst of rifle fire silenced the human voices and the mob dispersed. The Madras Regiment had come to our rescue. The Commanding Officer came to the flat. I explained to him what happened and begged to be taken to my sister (and guardian), an officer of Indian National Airways, who had been working round the clock to evacuate Muslims who wanted to migrate to a new homeland called Pakistan.

Wahid was in a state of shock when we broke open the toilet door and took him to my sister's office. She asked him if he would like to go to Pakistan. He nodded his head forlornly but said that he had no money. She paid his fare and I took him to the coach which would take him to the airport. He hugged me before boarding the bus. He took out a bunch of keys and handed them to me saying, 'Baba, my shop is now yours. Thank you for saving my life'.

As I watched the coach taking Wahid away from my life, I thought of my other friends who had been taken away by other coaches: Jamil, who joined me in standing up to a bigoted schoolmaster (and knocked me out in the boxing ring a little later), Kaiser, the brightest student, Habib, the bully; Salim, the class dunce. It didn't matter that your families knew each other for generations; it didn't matter that you were the closest friends; what mattered was that you were a Hindu or a Muslim; that you were an Indian or a Pakistani. Your life depended on it.

I was standing on the same balcony two years later when I saw a dishevelled man glance furtively towards the flat. I recognized Wahid and called him up. He took much longer than the moments he had taken when the mob was baying at his heels. He stood uncertainly at the door. Then he hugged me tightly. His tears percolated through the collar of my shirt.

Whilst my sister brewed tea for Wahid, I took out the keys of Wahid's shop from the cupboard and handed them to him. I also confessed that I had occasionally borrowed the green Raleigh. Wahid laughed. 'Baba,' he said, 'I gave the shop to you. So the Raleigh cycle as well as all the other cycles are rightfully yours.'

'No, Wahid,' said my sister who came in with the tea tray, 'we were only caretaking your shop.'

'In any case,' I piped in, 'the tyre has punctured!'

'Miss Sahib,' said Wahid to my sister, 'I had no money when I reached Karachi. I couldn't start a business or get a job. So I came back hoping that my brothers would help me. But they threw me out saying that I was a Pakistani. Yet you, a Hindu family, helped me to escape death and are now willing to give me another lease on life.'

'Wahid,' said my sister, 'it doesn't matter whether you are an Indian or a Pakistani; it doesn't matter whether we are Hindu or Muslim; it matters that you are a friend.'

Wahid sold his shop and his cycles. The green Raleigh remained as a memento of the friendship.

* * *

1954. Immediately on graduation from St Stephen's College (whose alumni include President Ziaul Haq of Pakistan), I volunteered to join a road building project at Musiari, a village near Murree. Sponsored by Service Civil Internationale, the camp had three volunteers from India and a dozen European conscientious objectors who had left their countries to avoid conscription.

The project started disastrously. Ashraf, the Pakistani Liaison Officer, did not arrive in time. Whilst the European volunteers were received with cheers and applause, the Indians were received with jeers and derision. Our haversacks were snatched from us. We were marched before the Village Headman. He asked why the Indians were there. He was sure that we were spies sent to operate in the vicinity of Murree, an important military base. I spoke to him in the best Urdu I could muster (we 'Dehlavis', or inhabitants of Delhi, call it Hindustani). I explained that we had come to build a road for them, and a bridge between nations—a proper road to prevent the villagers heavily laden with laundered clothes from falling from the narrow bridlepath—and that, symbolically, the Indian group consisted of a Hindu, a Muslim, and a Christian. I asked him where was that famous hospitality of our two countries which did not distinguish Black from White; Indian from Pakistani; Hindu from Muslim? The old man closed his eyes for a couple of minutes. He then began to speak about Delhi, which he had visited frequently in the past; of Jama Masjid and the Red Fort; of his relatives in Chandni Chowk, Lal Kuan and Nizamuddin; of the millions of common bonds. He ordered a goat to be killed; a feast to be held; local youth to help the project.

The road was built in a record time of three months.

* * *

1961. I was visiting the Ikramullah home. Arrival at Clifton was homecoming at its best. While Inam, Salma, and Naz were at work and Bitlum (now Crown Princess of Jordan) was at school, Uncle Ikram, Aunty Soghra, and I would exchange memories. Uncle Ikram, who was recuperating from a heart attack, and I would quarrel about who would read which 'comic' first.

One day Uncle Ikram received a letter from his youngest brother, Hidayatullah (Uncle Haddi to us), who was Chief

Justice of the Maharashtra High Court and who had been elevated to the Supreme Court Bench. Uncle Haddi had written, 'I do not know whether it is better to be a big fish in a small pond or a small fish in a big pond'. Uncle Ikram replied, '...it does not matter whether you are a big fish or small fish. You must do your best for your country—as I must do for mine. Who knows, you may one day become the President of India...'

Uncle Haddi was twice Acting President of India.

* * *

1987. The phone rang. My teenage daughter picked up the receiver. A lady asked for Pandu Chintamani. Nilam, my daughter, said I was out and asked if she could take a message.

The lady said, 'My name is Naz...'

Nilam interrupted, 'Are you Naz Ikramullah?'

'Yes', said Naz, 'My husband, Ashraf, our daughter Amna, and I are passing through Delhi. But how did you guess I was Naz Ikramullah?'

'Because Daddy is constantly telling us about his adoptive family: Uncle Ikram, Aunty Soghra, Inam, Salma, Naz, and Bitlum,' replied Nilam.

It did not matter that she had left India forty years earlier; it did not matter that I had not met (or even corresponded with) her for over twenty-six years; what mattered was that a sister had come looking for her brother.

The Ikramullah family perhaps epitomizes a heritage that transcends the boundaries that divide the subcontinent into three nations: a Pakistani son, a Bangladeshi daughter, a Canadian-Indian daughter, and a Jordanian daughter. And an adoptive son too, who is proud to be an Indian, who is proud to be a Hindu, who, most of all, is proud to be an extension of a Pakistani Muslim family.

As the post-monsoon harvest season begins, the festival of Raksha Bandhan is celebrated. Sisters tie *Rakhis* on their brothers' wrists and the brothers pledge to protect their sisters forever. Legend has it that Rani Padmini tied the *Rakhi* on the wrist of Emperor Allaudin Khilji. And every year, without fail, two envelopes arrive with *Rakhis*—Naz's *Rakhi* to me and Amna's *Rakhi* to my son.

For that is tradition. That is a manifestation of the common heritage.

Aruna Asaf Ali

Daughter of Upendra Nath Gangulee of Calcutta, Aruna Asaf Ali was in the front rank of Indian freedom fighters. Barely out of her teens, she met and married Asaf Ali in 1928 at Naini Tal, and was inducted into public service shortly thereafter. In Delhi, where her husband was a barrister and a senior leader of the Indian National Congress, she set about organizing the Delhi Women's League, and later rose to the top echelons of Congress leadership herself. However, when the Congress passed the 'Quit India' resolution in 1942 and launched a non-violent resistance movement against the British Raj, she joined the party's Forward Bloc and along with a number of other young Congress activists, remained underground until the end of World War II.

As president of the Delhi State Congress Committee, she developed strong ideological differences with the Congress mainstream, particularly over the partition scheme, and did not approve of her husband accepting the appointment as Ambassador to the United States shortly before independence. Even after she joined him in Washington, she openly criticized the anti-Soviet policies of the US and spent much time lecturing in Mexico and other neighbouring countries. Drawn more and more to the politics of the left, she was actively associated with the Congress Socialist Party and founded a weekly, *Janata*. With the support of the Socialists and the Communist Party of India, she was elected the first mayor of Delhi after independence.

Until her death in 1996, she was chairperson of the *Patriot* group of newspapers.

The Bhakti-Sufi Legacy

Aruna Asaf Ali

The friendly encounter of the egalitarian and reforming movement of Hindu devotional Bhakti and of the Sufi sages and mystics, who started arriving in India from the twelfth century, is a major event in history. It is perhaps the most precious part of the subcontinent's cultural legacy, though like any heritage it needs to be creatively reinterpreted and renewed from time to time to accommodate the changing material and political conditions of human life.

Discrimination based on hereditary caste, that peculiar bane of Hindu society, was condemned by the leaders of the Bhakti movement. The Sufis taught, by precept and example, the need to overcome the tendency to fanaticism in Islam. Both repudiated the subordination of women common to Hindu and Muslim society.

I recall how my husband used to remark on the difference that might have been made to the history of India had Akbar's grandson Shah Jahan been succeeded by the liberal-minded Dara Shikoh rather than Aurangzeb. Dara Shikoh made a rendering into Persian of selections from the Upanishads, regarded as the culmination of the Vedas, under the title *Sirr-i-Akbar* (The Great Secret). It was from a Latin and subsequently French translation of this work of Dara Shikoh that the West came to know the Upanishads for the first time. Professor M. Mujeeb, who used to teach at Jamia Millia, established in the early 1920s as a nationalist alternative to the British-patronized Muslim educational centre at Aligarh, says in his book, *The Indian Muslims*:

What he (Dara) represents socially is the culmination of that understanding between Muslims and non-Muslims of which Akbar laid the foundation...The translation of the *Upanishads* was not due to literary curiosity, like the translations of the *Mahabharata* and the *Ramayana* and other works of Sanskrit literature made in Akbar's time and earlier; it was the result of a passionate search for truth.

Dara Shikoh expounded in the *Majma-ul-Bahrain* (The Mingling of the Two Oceans) the fundamental unity of the teachings of Hinduism and Islam, observing that the difference was only in terminology. This work has been preserved in the Persian as well as in a Sanskrit version known as *Samudra-sangama-grantha*. No wonder that K. R. Qanungo, a biographer of Dara Shikoh, said:

> Anyone who intends to take up the solution of the problem of religious peace in India must begin the work where Dara had left it, and proceed on the path chalked out by that prince.[1]

Maulana Abul Kalam Azad, with whom my husband was closely associated during the freedom struggle, wrote in 1910 in an essay on the seventeenth century mystic Sarmad, who was executed on Aurangzeb's order shortly after the killing of Dara Shikoh:

> During the last days of Emperor Shah Jahan, Dara Shikoh was heir-apparent...From his early years Dara displayed the attributes of a dervish. He always kept company with philosophers and Sufis...The humility with which Dara met the Muslim divines was matched by the devotion with which he bowed his head before the Hindu saints and *sadhus*. Who can deny the purity of this principle? Because in this exalted state of mind, if one can still disguish between *Kufr* and Islam, then what is the difference between blindness and vision?[2]

(Later, however, Maulana Azad in his *Tarjuman*, a translation of and commentary on the Koran which he wrote during his internment at Ranchi till the end of 1919, interpreted the tolerance of the Koran to 'include all forms of monotheism', thus excluding popular Hinduism which is polytheistic and pantheistic.)

What made the Indian soil congenial to the religious synthesis symbolized by Dara Shikoh? How is it that Muslim Sufis were welcomed by people of another faith? G. N. S. Raghavan, in the course of a full-length biography of my husband[3] that is to be published shortly, suggests that it is accounted for by a long tradition of cultural synthesis:

> Though the Aryan-Dravidian encounter that began around 2000 BC had been initially hostile, it developed into a synthesis, with much racial mixing. The religion that emerged from this interaction was designated by outsiders as Hinduism because of the name 'Hindu' given by them to the people of the land of the river Sindhu (pronounced in Persian with an aspirate), or Indus (*Indos* in Greek) from which the name India is derived. This religion of India, spanning the sub-continent from the Himalayas to Kanyakumari at the southern tip, had a certain measure of tolerance built into it if only because of the multiplicity of gods and goddesses. It is typical of the Indian gift of syncretism that Parvati, wife of the pre-Aryan deity Siva, was declared to be and is worshipped to this day as the sister of the Aryan deity Vishnu.

A humanism entailing compassion for the needy, and transcending differences of race and caste, finds utterance as early as in Vedic literature spanning a thousand years from about 1500 BC. In the Rig Veda are found lines which counsel man to be compassionate to his kind:

> Fortune, like two chariot wheels revolving, now to one man comes nigh, now to another. Who has the power should give unto the needy. One who feeds all by himself sins all by himself.

Yagnavalkya (about 700 BC) deprecates the concept of high and low according to the accident of birth:

> It is not our religion, still less the colour of our skin, that produces virtue; virtue must be practised. Therefore, let no one do to others what he would not have done to himself.

In the Chandogya Upanishad, Svetaketu is advised by his father:

> Live the disciplined life of a student of sacred knowledge. No one, indeed, belonging to our family is unlearned in the Vedas and remains a Brahmin only by family connections as it were.[4]

The earliest of the reformist schools of the religion of India were Jainism, founded by Vardhamana Mahavira (599-527 BC) and Buddhism, by Siddhartha Gautama (563-483 BC). Both were egalitarian and admitted women to their orders. The basic beliefs of both were the same and are illustrated by the following excerpts from the vast body of Buddhist texts:

> No Brahmin is such by birth;
> No outcast is such by birth.
> An outcast is such by his deeds;
> A Brahmin is such by his deeds.

> There are ten ways of the Boddhisattva (Being of Wisdom):
> He will give up his body and his life but not the Law of Righteousness.
> He bows humbly to all beings, and does not increase in pride.
> He has compassion for the weak and does not dislike them.
> He gives the best food to those who are hungry.
> He protects those who are afraid.
> He strives for the healing of those who are sick.
> He benefits the poor with his riches.
> He repairs the shrines of the Buddha with plaster.
> He speaks to all beings pleasingly.
> He bears the burdens of those who are tired and weary.

In south India, a poet of the Sangam age of Tamil literature (ascribed to the second and third centuries AD) affirmed:

Every city is my city; all people are my people.
Life's good comes not from others' gift, nor ill;
Likewise, pain and relief from pain are one's own.

Tirvuvalluvar, of the fifth century, born in a supposedly low caste, wrote a string of ethical verses known as the Kural. He affirmed:

The living soul subsists in love;
The loveless are but skin and bone.
He alone lives who knows that he is one with all;
The rest have their place among the dead.

The sayings of an eleventh-century woman sage, Avvai, are regarded by Tamils as the quintessence of wisdom. There is an ethical injunction of Avvai by which to teach children each vowel of the alphabet.

Equality of the sexes was affirmed most forcefully by some of the sages of the Bhakti movement in Karnataka, a rich crop of poet-saints who have been described as 'great voices of a sweeping movement of protest and reform in Hindu society'. Basava wrote:

Sometimes I am man,
sometimes I am woman.
O lord of the meeting rivers,
I'll make war for you
but I'll be your devotees' bride.

And Devara Dasimayya wrote:

If they see
breasts and long hair coming, they call it woman;
if beard and whiskers

they call it man:
but, look, the self that hovers
in between
is neither man
nor woman.

Against this background of the Bhakti movement's religious and social humanism, battling against the male chauvinism and irrationality of orthodoxy, it is no wonder that the Sufi sages who came to India were met with popular welcome. One of the earliest was Khwaja Moin-ud-din Chishti born in Persia, who reached India in 1191 and, after staying for some time in Delhi, settled down at Ajmer. Hailed as *Gharib Nawaz* (Friend of the Needy), he is venerated to this day and his *dargah* attracts both Muslim and Hindu devotees. 'If God has given you eyes,' he said, 'you will see that all paths lead to Him.'

Baba Farid of the thirteenth century said: 'Discard costly garments. The Lord is met in poor dress.' In 1268 Baba Farid named as his successor his disciple Nizamuddin Aulia who chose Ghyaspur, at that time a secluded place about six miles from the walled city of Delhi, as his abode for prayer and meditation. The place is now in the heart of the metropolis and is known as Nizamuddin. 'Nothing will bring greater reward on the day of judgement,' Khwaja Nizamuddin Aulia said, 'than bringing happiness to the hearts of men.'

Among my husband's close friends was Khwaja Hasan Nizami, the hereditary chief of the *dargah* and a noted writer in Urdu. Asaf Ali had no strong religious inclination in the conventional sense, but shared the Bhakti-Sufi values of tolerance, goodwill, and compassion. The catholicity of Asaf Ali's humanism was a further extension, in the conditions of his time, of the Bhakti-Sufi spirit. As G. N. S. Raghavan says:

He was receptive to all of the three great streams of the heritage of human thought and culture to which he was heir: that of India, his native land, right from Vedic times; of Islam, his natal religion, and of the Bhakti-Sufi movement of the medieval period in which indigenous, pre-Islamic humanism and Islamic humanism reinforced each other; and, finally, the encounter with the West, political and cultural, which was the central factor in shaping the personality and values of many of the best Indians during the twentieth century.

By 1928, the year in which Asaf Ali and I met (in January, at Allahabad) and married (in September, at Naini Tal), there had been a breakdown of the harmonious relations between the two major religious communities of India that Bhakti-Sufism had made possible. Aurangzeb's policies had alienated the majority of his non-Muslim subjects who were made to pay a jiziya tax, and had embroiled him in wars with the Rajputs, the Sikhs, and the Marathas. This made India vulnerable to Western colonial penetration. When the British emerged victorious from the competition between European powers for control of India, they did everything to keep Hindus and Muslims divided. The partition of Bengal in 1905 was part of the design. Though the partition was annulled in 1911, the introduction of separate electorates for Muslims under the Indian Councils Act of 1909 ensured that India would thence forward be socially and politically divided.

Mahatma Gandhi thought in 1919 that he could bring about Hindu-Muslim unity by offering Hindu support to the pan-Islamic cause of Khilafat. But the euphoria generated by this movement proved short-lived. It ended with a reaction of Hindu-Muslim rioting in various parts of India, culminating in the murder in Delhi by a Muslim fanatic, towards the close of 1926, of Swami Shradhhanand, a leader of the Arya Samaj.

Against this background, our marriage touched off a storm of protest. Proclaiming himself my guardian

following the death of my father Upendra Nath Gangulee
in March 1928, his brother Nagendra Nath Gangulee (an
agricultural scientist who was a member of the Royal
Commission on Agriculture) shot off a telegram to the
District Magistrate of Naini Tal that I was a minor and did
not have his consent to marry Asaf Ali. My uncle went so
far as to proclaim to his relatives and friends that Aruna
was dead so far as he was concerned, and he had performed
her *shraddh*. (It is a different matter that, some years later
when he met Asaf in Delhi, at my instance, Nagendra Nath
Gangulee was fascinated by my husband and the two
became good friends). On the side of Asaf Ali's family, too,
the immediate reactions to his maverick action were
adverse.

Outside the familial network, reactions were largely
hostile. Pandit Madan Mohan Malaviya would turn his face
away from me when we were thrown together at Congress
gatherings because, although he was a social reformer who
promoted women's education, he could not endure the
thought of a Bengali Brahmin girl marrying a Muslim.
When Asaf Ali stood as Congress candidate for election to
the Central Legislative Assembly from Delhi (which was a
rare instance of a general constituency not earmarked for
either Muslim or non-Muslim candidates), communalists
both Hindu and Muslim held it against him that he had
married a Hindu.

Tallest among those in public life who blessed the
unorthodox marriage stood Mahatma Gandhi. He did not
believe in inter-communal marriage as a means of bringing
about Hindu-Muslim unity; rather, he thought that such
marriages could only follow unity. Nevertheless he was
happy about the marriage. He spoke of it as a symbol of
Hindu-Muslim unity. I protested that I had married Asaf
not because he was a Muslim but because of the affinity we
felt, with our shared interest in English literature and the
impression he made on me with his knowledge of history
and philosophy, his agreeable personality, and refined

manners. But Gandhiji insisted that our marriage had symbolic significance. C. Rajagopalachari, Maulana Azad, and Khwaja Hasan Nizami were among the friends of Asaf Ali who blessed the marriage.

Among family friends closer to me in age was Shaista Ikramullah. I have not come across a better summing up of Asaf Sahib's personality than her appreciative reference in her autobiography *(From Purdah to Parliament,* Cresset Press, London, 1963):

> Mr Asaf Ali was not only one of the most prominent figures of the Indian national movement but one of the most charming also. He belonged to Delhi, not only in the sense that he came from one of its oldest families, but because he was the quintessence of its culture. He had the courtesy and the charm, the grace, the elegance and the manner, that undefinable air of breeding which only those nurtured in the best tradition of our culture possess. I have never heard and never shall hear again Urdu spoken as Asaf Ali spoke it. It makes me sad to think that my children have not even heard the full range of its musical cadence. I was indeed fortunate to have heard it, fortunate to have known persons of such rare quality as Asaf Ali...

Asaf Ali, like Maulana Azad and other nationalists, rejected the two-nation theory which was a total repudiation of the Bhakti-Sufi tradition. But Asaf Ali recognized that there could be no forced union if a large body of people wanted to separate from the rest. As early as 1941 he envisaged the possibility of partition and also looked beyond that; to a co-operative relationship between the separated parts of the subcontinent. From Gujarat jail in Punjab, where he was detained for his participation in the Individual *Satyagraha* against a subject India being dragged by the British into World War II, Asaf Ali wrote in May 1941 to his friend Mulla Wahidi, editor of the literary magazine *Adib,* suggesting that a corner may be reserved for some of the essays he was writing on India's composite culture:

> India may remain one or may be divided into Hindustan and Pakistan, but the importance of this composite culture will remain. Even if the country is divided into ten pieces, the composite culture will compel the neighbours to live and let live. Even if they fight, they will have to come to terms one day with the map of this composite culture.
>
> If you have a collection of Iqbal before you, just have a look at the poems on Rama and Nanak. In addition, kindly see certain parts of *Tasveer-e-Dard*. If you come across any more of such poetry, please let me know. I am thinking of compiling an anthology of such poems.
>
> I am having a look at Faizi's translation of the *Geeta*. There are hundreds of couplets in it which a Muslim cannot for a moment disown. The religion of the Sufis is of the same genre. Here there is a confluence of Hindustan and Islamistan. This aspect is worth bringing out.

The two-nation theory, which held that the Muslims of the Indian subcontinent constituted one nation and the Hindus another, seemed to stand proved in 1947, only to be disproved in 1971 when the eastern wing of Pakistan broke away and became a separate, sovereign Bangladesh. Recent developments in the erstwhile USSR and Yugoslavia have further demonstrated that there can be no forced unions in this age of democracy and self-determination. Equally, the formation of the South Asian Association for Regional Co-operation (SAARC), among whose members are India, Pakistan, and Bangladesh, and of a Commonwealth of Independent States comprising most of the former constituents of the Soviet Union, indicate a recognition of the need for regional co-operation between neighbours.

With remarkable forevision, Asaf Ali envisaged co-operation between sovereign units in the Indian subcontinent after the exercise of self-determination. He wrote in his Prison Diary at Ahmadnagar Fort:

13th October 1942. With goodwill, Hindus and Muslims, if they do not settle down as members of the same nation, can be allies knitted together in common economic bonds, with equal dignity and opportunity for peaceful achievement. Our watchword should be: 'Live and let live in a free and dignified family of mankind.'

14th March 1944. I am convinced on practical grounds that by far the best course for India as a whole is...recognition of the principle of self-determination by homogenous communities or national groups. It will mean a willing partnership by all, or by as many as see a clear community of interest in a confederal grouping. But there should be no forced union, for it will spell obstruction and internal weakness. If there has to be a Pakistan, a treaty will have to be negotiated by it with Hindustan. It should be a treaty stipulating political and commercial collaboration for mutual benefit.

15th August 1944. Let India as a whole be looked upon as a 'Commonwealth' of peoples or nations. If the British Commonwealth can subsist and act together in spite of different sovereign political structures of the Dominions, why cannot India do the same? Surely, if independent Nepal and the sovereign native States can exist side by side and within the political system of the British Empire, they as well as other constituents can do the same as distinct and sovereign structures within the political system of an Indian Commonwealth.

It is true that economic planning on an India-wide scale, and Defence, will require much closer co-operation than the sovereignty of the parts of an Indian Commonwealth may entitle one to presume. But surely, if the British Empire could devise means of common defence and economic preferences, so can an Indian Commonwealth.

All this can happen, given goodwill and mutual trust and recognition of larger common interests. It is a pity that our statesmen and politicians think in no terms other than what they have been taught by their rulers to employ. They talk in terms of choice only between federation and partition. The logic which appeals to controversialists is the destructive-analytical, not the constructive-synthetic.

14th October 1944. Blind sentiment rooted in history seems to have proved too strong for a confident and united bid for freedom. Perhaps not until Hindustan and Pakistan have actually worked as free countries for some time will either Hindus or Muslims and others begin to see things in proper perspective. If so, well, let even a divided India begin to function as a co-operative commonwealth of sovereign states.

By an interesting coincidence, as I was preparing this article in collaboration with G. N. S. Raghavan, the first meeting was held in New Delhi, on 4 May 1992, of SAARC's Inter-Governmental Group on Trade Liberalization. The meeting considered measures to dismantle tariff and non-tariff barriers in the way of free flow of trade between member countries. One may perhaps hope that this will mark the beginning of the triumph of common sense over political prejudice. Over the decades, as Ram Jethmalani pointed out in an article in *The Indian Express* on 21 February 1992, Pakistan preferred to buy coal at higher prices from China, Poland, and Australia rather than from India; similarly with tractors and tube-well motors, bicycles, etc. which can be had cheaper from India if only because of the saving in transport cost. India for its part, says Jethmalani, can save a substantial amount by importing raw cotton, wool, and oilseeds from Pakistan rather than sources farther away.

While entertaining the hope that SAARC might help the countries to move towards Asaf Ali's vision of a sub-continental commonwealth, the desired co-operation will prove durable only if it is based on the Bhakti-Sufi spirit of human brotherhood, which Jawaharlal Nehru translated into the idiom of the modern age as peaceful and co-operative co-existence. It is remarkable that the Bhakti-Sufi legacy has been valued not only by persons of my husband's generation but by others of later times. For instance Khwaja Ahmad Abbas (born a quarter-century after Asaf Ali), writes in his autobiography[6] about the Sufi saint Bu Ali Shah 'Qalander' of Panipat (where Ahmad Abbas was born):

> Legend has it that the saint died at a lonely place which was equidistant from Panipat, Karnal and Kunjpura. So the people from all these three places turned up to claim the body, for the town where the saint was buried would be blessed forever. They started quarrelling and fighting about who had prior claim upon the dead saint, but when they lifted the ragged sheet that lay over him, they discovered only a pile of flowers. So each party took one third of the flowers and buried it in their own place. This sort of thing is also supposed to have happened when Kabir died, and there was a tussle between Hindus and Muslims as to whether his body would be burnt or buried. To me these legends, like most of religious lore, have only a symbolic significance as the ancients' way to teach the ethics of humanism to the simple people through poetic parables. But I am rather struck by the secular and proletarian affinities of the Sufi saints and their ready acceptance by the Muslim and the Hindu masses.

The continuing relevance of the Bhakti-Sufi heritage for ending strife in the name of religion is brought out by a leading Indian Muslim journalist, Saeed Naqvi, in the course of an article in *Patriot* of 24 May 1990. He wrote it as a response to a speech delivered by Lal Krishna Advani, the Bharatiya Janata Party leader, at a gathering of volunteers of the Rashtriya Swayamsevak Sangh at Coimbatore in South India. Naqvi says towards the close of the article:

> But everything is not lost. Yes, folks in Jama Masjid (Delhi) and Charminar (Hyderabad) and Malappuram[7] are evolving outside the pale of the Ramayana. Just as the Swayamsevaks you addressed in Coimbatore are growing up without any knowledge of Dara Shikoh. If this continues, we shall have

institutionalised apartheid...It does not have to be that way. Traditions and customs that are dear to you and me are alive in India.

The continuing strength of these traditions was strikingly demonstrated during the telecast by Doordarshan, India's television network, in the late 1980s of the widely-popular serial on the *Mahabharata* epic. The script was written by a Muslim, the Urdu poet Rahim Masoom Reza. Let me conclude this article with some more extracts from the writing of Asaf Ali on the theme of India's composite culture, and of the wider human heritage of the world's art, literature, and thought to which we are heirs:

> Shorn of their complex religious ritual, Diwali, Bhaiyaduj (Raksha Bandhan), Basant and Holi were adopted by the Mughals and adapted to the growth of a common Indo-Mughal culture. In any case, I need not apologize for interesting myself in a Hindu festival, for I see no reason why Hindus, Muslims, Christians, Sikhs and rationalists in India should not participate in one another's festivities without necessarily sharing one another's religious beliefs.
>
> I was born a Muslim, and I have almost since the age of fifteen or sixteen steadily re-examined, evaluated and sifted the fundamentals from the rituals and dogmatic assertions in every quarter. Philosophy and science were my favourite subjects at college, and have remained so. This has helped me to what I hope is a just appreciation and assessment of the basic concern of all religions with the rules of human conduct. While one should scrupulously steer clear of irrational, superstitious and degenerate distortions and practices, which reduce religions to travesties of the purer essence, one can always win respect and toleration for one's own beliefs and faith by a liberal appreciation and understanding of others.
>
> For a rationalist, who can be nothing but a humble seeker after truth and light, it is all the more imperative to be gentle in rejection, magnanimous in appreciation, and yet remain firm like a rock against the erosive waves of ignorant superstition and unreasoning fanaticism.

In what may be described as the backward glance of science and rationalism, the history of religions presents a most fascinating subject. The human mind appears to have moved from plane to plane of thought in a close spiral, each subsequent plane of thought lying a level above the preceding one, but each resembling the former almost to the point of identity.

The three main areas and sources of development are the Egypto-Greek (including the Babylonian and Assyrian), Semitic and Indo-Chinese. Of course it is possible to sub-divide them. I lump the Iranian with the Indo-Chinese. Throughout the last five or six thousand years the tendency has been to fix the precise relationship of man with the rest of the universe. Hence the journey from polytheism to monotheism and then a pantheism—I mean the Sufi and Vedantic pantheism, not the grosser and narrower pantheism of Rome. All this signifies a remarkable mental development and most creditable simplification of the complex phenomena that is the Universe.

But, cast far apart in distant portions of the globe, men have failed to adjust the most essential relationship, i.e., between themselves. They should have begun by discovering and establishing human unity before anything else. They have tried to do it through religions, and failed. And they have fallen back on the primitive urges—racial and national narrowness. Sometimes one hears that 'language' can be a common bond: can it? This is another delusion.

A humane morality, by which I mean values based on the recognition of equal economic needs and rights of all human beings is, to my mind, the objective towards which mankind has to travel to get over the periodic distress through which the world has had to go. But I fear that the desired consummation is still a distant goal. The wise idealist is one who discourages optimism and consequently impatience. Nature has had to crawl at a snail's pace for hundreds of millions of years to produce man; and man has laboured for at least half a million years to come to his present state. Ideas are always centuries in advance of the existing conditions. Realists, therefore, accept ideals as guides but never lose a sense of proportion, and make the best of the hard logic of reality.

Religion is ennobling when it is practised by those who have tried to understand the deeper and profounder purposes underlying it. But it can be incredibly debasing when it is relied upon by narrow-minded bigots and unreasoning zealots. I fear much of the world is writhing in the hands of the latter.

I remember a friend of mine once saying (and he was otherwise an intellectual):[8] 'The most estimable man who does not profess my religion cannot be equal to the most despicable of my co-religionists.' And I heard once the identical assertion based on colour. These are man's weak and blind spots. Some day he will get rid of them and make the human family happier and better. Meanwhile those who feel and know these things must hold their souls in patience, and pray that God's sublimating processes may rescue humanity from its follies and sins.

If humanity is thought of as a whole, as it should be, the achievements of the great men—sages, poets, saints and intellectual giants—not merely of one race or one place but of all races and of all places, are the proud heritage of all human beings. Therefore I would like to see the present generation of the human race nurtured on this universal heritage so that a healthy international outlook is created. Only thus can the ideal of a society of rational human beings, wedded to progress, be realized.

I feel quite as thrilled when a beautiful poem or a profound thought, or a fine piece of art or anything else of a sublime nature comes before me out of the past, whether it is out of ancient Egypt or China, India or Chaldea, Greece or Rome, Persia or Arabia, as when I come across anything modern and elevating, whether out of the West or the East. The moment anyone expresses a preference on racial or national grounds, it sounds to me narrow. Thought, beauty and practical achievements are universal, and they should be the heritage of all.

If I have quoted extensively from Asaf Ali, it is because he thought deeply on the theme of this volume, even as he himself was an embodiment of the good elements in the composite cultural heritage of the people of the subcontinent, and of the wider world.

NOTES

1. Quoted in *An Advanced History of India* (p. 481) by R. C. Majumdar and others, Macmillan, 1950.
2. Quoted by President R. Venkataraman in the course of the Azad Memorial Lecture delivered by him in New Delhi on 7 May 1992.
3. Titled *M. Asaf Ali: Portrait of a Humanist,* the biography was commissioned by the Delhi Administration as part of its contribution to the observance of the birth centenaries of Jawaharlal Nehru and others who were born in the 1880s.
4. *Sources of Indian Tradition* compiled by Theodore de Bary and others, Motilal Banarasidas, 1963.
5. *Speaking of Siva* by A. K. Remanujan, Penguin, 1973. (pp. 3-13).
6. *I am not an Island*, Vikas Publishing House, 1977.
7. Carved out as a Muslim-majority district in Kerala, in 1969 when a Communist-led government, in coalition with the Muslim League, was in power.
8. The reference is apparently to Maulana Mohammad Ali, who said: 'As a follower of Islam I am bound to regard the creed of Islam as superior to that professed by the followers of any non-Islamic religion. And in this sense the creed of even a fallen and degraded Mussalman is entitled to a higher place than that of any other non-Muslim irrespective of his high character, even though the person in question be Mahatma Gandhi himself.'

Mukhtar Zaman

Mukhtar Zaman was born in February 1924 in Bijnor, UP, India. He took his LL.B. and MA English degrees from the University of Allahabad. He began his journalistic career in 1947 with the *Morning News* of Calcutta, and one of his first assignments was to cover the birth of Pakistan in Dhaka (then East Pakistan). He worked for papers and news agencies in Dhaka until 1953, when he joined the *Toledo Blade* in Ohio USA, and later joined the staff of Reuters and BBC in London.

Upon his return to Pakistan, he resumed work with the Associated Press of Pakistan (APP) and held several important positions including Director-General, APP, and Director (Asia), International Association of Islamic Banks.

A respected journalist, he has travelled around the world and covered events of historic importance. Prior to the Islamic Summit of 1974, he met and interviewed leaders from the Middle East and Northern Africa.

He has taught Journalism for several years, and is the author of several humorous essays in Urdu, and over 200 articles on historical, social, political, and literary subjects in Urdu and English.

He is married to Professor Salmana Zaman, and lives in Karachi.

Hindu-Muslim Cultural Relations Before Partition

Mukhtar Zaman

Cultural relations between Hindus and Muslims had for centuries tended to be normal, namely that of the ruler and the ruled. Muslim rulers, like other absolute sovereign powers of the time all over the world, dealt with their supporters and opponents, Hindus and Muslims, alike, irrespective of their religion. The advent of the British Raj, and the gradually changing political climate, raised the question of 'numbers'. Personal politico-cultural rule was gone and a future democratic set-up was promised. The British Raj, the steps towards western democracy, constitutionalism, changing times, and full-scale media publicity raised the question of 'numbers', which naturally favoured the majority community, the Hindus. So the Muslims and the Hindus drifted slowly apart politically—a logical corollary of a democratic but inevitable polity. This naturally meant cultural distance. It had to happen, because it was the logical, natural course, and any study of pre-partition Hindu-Muslim relations must take this into account. To come to a dispassionate conclusion, we must study the subject in its entirety with all the changing standards of socio-political attitudes over the years. First let us look at the background.

The Background

Way back in AD 712 Mohammad Bin Qasim was the first Muslim to set foot in India. He took over Sindh, but he and his companions soon started building bridges between the two great communities. He had Sanskrit books translated into Arabic and started a humane politico-cultural system. This was the first cultural step towards a friendship for Hinduism.

The process was then halted for some two and a half centuries, until Mahmood Ghaznavi's onslaughts and later those of Mohammad Ghori, whose descendants made permanent homes in India. Politics played its part. One regime succeeded the other—Khiljis, Tughlaqs, Syeds, Suris, Lodhis, and Mughals all fought for supremacy. But all of them had two things in common: (a) they all regarded India as their home and settled down here for good, and (b) all of them patronized Persian, which became the official language but which in time gave way to Urdu. Persian was foreign to this land but it adapted, changing its colour according to the environment. Amir Khusro was a Persian poet who drew inspiration from Khaqani and Saadi, but he did not hesitate to use Indian words like *Mumani* and *dahi* or equivocation like *Dur Dur Mua*. He was the first Indian poet who can be said to have laid the foundations of the Urdu language. Ghalib was also a great Persian poet and naturally quoted *Ustads* of Iran in support of his phraseology, but his fame rests mainly on his Urdu poetry and his letters in Urdu prose which, it may be noted, he wrote to hundreds of Hindu and Muslim friends, pupils, and colleagues. His father and uncle served as military commanders under both Muslim rulers and Hindu Rajas.

An Indian scholar rightly says that Islam preached the equality of men, which initially brought Hindus and Muslims closer to each other. Sufis respected Hindu gods and goddesses. But as time progressed Muslims left their pristine simplicity and developed a caste system along the lines of the Hindu system. The Mughals in particular adopted many practices for births, marriages, deaths, etc., which were Hindu in origin. Even the last king, Bahadur Shah Zafar, on the occasion of *Dussehra*, released a *neel kanth,* a bird with blue feathers associated by the Hindus with *Dussehra* rites. This had nothing to do with Islam. Islam had long ceased to be the simple, straightforward religion that the Prophet (PBUH) had preached in Arabia. Islam and Muslim culture reached India via Iran, and in India it found an even more complex society. There it borrowed many rites and even superstitions from Hindu culture.

Urdu

Urdu was a strong cultural link between the Muslim and Hindu communities. It was at the time of Hazrat Nizamuddin Auliya, some 700 years ago, that Urdu first started developing. It is said that the saint once questioned the audience as to what had they done to develop a language that could form a link between the two communities. He said that he and his people had settled in India for good and that it had become necessary that they should have a common language so that he could communicate with the common people who were his audience. Khusro thereupon recited some of his poems containing local words. It may be only a story, but it has some basis which cannot be denied. (Rajkumar Hardev, Khusro's pupil, wrote *Nizam Bansi*).

It is true that the Tughlaqs, Khiljis, and Mughals, etc., used Persian, but Urdu slowly made its way. By the time of Jehangir and Shahjehan we find that Urdu had become the language of the common people in the northern belt.

In the south, cultural affinity began with the setting up of five Sultanates: Qutub Shahi in Golkunda, Nizam Shahi in Ahmadnagar, Adil Shahi in Bijapur, Barid Shahi in Beedar and Imdad Shahi in Berar. The transfer of the capital city from Delhi to Daulatabad (Devgiri) by Mohammad Tughlaq had an indirect cultural effect. Hundreds of citizens of Delhi moved to the south and took with them their own languages, which were akin to Urdu.

In due course of time, *amir saddas*—one leader of every 100 families—were appointed. They settled in the south and made Urdu the common denominator and their chief vehicle of expression. This is how the cultural influence of the north reached the south. By the time the Mughals came, India was populated by an Urdu-speaking public. Persian continued to be the court language, but Urdu, or Hinduwi, Gujri, or Raikhta, as it was called at various stages and in manifold regions, became the means of the common man's communication in northern and southern India.

In the time of Jahangir and Shahjehan, the major poet was Mohammad Afzal Jhanjanvi, who wrote the *Bara Massa Bikat Kahani*. The last Mughal king, Bahadur Shah Zafar, was himself a well-known Urdu poet who claimed the pupilship of Zauq and later Ghalib. The latter was a major poet of Urdu, although he said, 'My Urdu collection of verses is colourless; if you really want to see what colour means, see my Persian poetry.' Little did he realize that it would mainly be his Urdu works for which he would be remembered.

History indicates that both the Muslims and the Hindus regarded the coming of the Muslims to India as something not unnatural. After all, Aryans had come earlier. But it should be underlined that, like the Aryans, the Muslims settled down in India and made it their home. All the Sufis, poets, learned men, historians, writers became a part of Indian society. Nazeer Akbarabadi wrote poetry eulogizing Hindu and Sikh saints, their rites and customs. Men like Ibrahim Lodhi and Raana Sange fought hand in hand against 'foreigners' like the Mughals. But once they were in, differences narrowed down and eventually disappeared because the 'foreigners' became 'Indians', so much so that Bahadur Shah Zafar became the symbol of unity.

The British Raj and the Fight for Freedom

The British were different. They took away raw materials, wealth, manuscripts, and souvenirs from India but never settled down here. They imposed their own language and culture but did not invent one. They created a gulf between the Hindus and Muslims and ruled them both with an iron hand. They were the first to raise the issue of Hindu and Muslim cultures as separate entities. A resolution making Hindi the court language of India, issued by a British Governor, Sir Anthony McDonnel, provoked Sir Syed and Mohsin-ul-Mulk. Sir Syed called it a 'political move'.

The fight for freedom began against this background. It should have been a 'joint venture'. Indeed the 1857 onslaught, known as the Sepoy Mutiny by the British and the First War of Independence by Indians and Pakistanis, was one instance where Hindu sepoys fought shoulder to shoulder with their Muslim compatriots. Their sovereign and central figure was Bahadur Shah Zafar, who had little power outside the Red Fort but who was a great sentimental symbol for both Hindus and Muslims.

The British rulers who won this fight against the forces of resistance exploited the situation. They divided the Hindus and Muslims on politico-religious grounds. There had always been differences in their outlook on life between Hindus and Muslims, but the co-existence of two separate religio-social entities was a foregone conclusion under the Mughals. They had learned to co-exist during the previous 800 years or so. We know that Muslims and Hindus fought the new Muslim invaders together. Once it was realized that the newcomers had settled in India, they were gradually accepted. The Muslims never felt inferior to the Hindu majority. Yet they did not overlook the achievement of Indians in the field of music, mathematics, philosophy, etc. In fact the Muslims publicized them and conveyed these ideas to Baghdad, Madina, and the cities of Central Asia through translations and travellers' writings.

We learn from history that besides a common language
the Muslims had developed a taste for Indian food,
cultivated a variety of fruits, learnt many arts. But the crux
of the problem was that they refused to merge with Indian
society.

It has rightly been remarked that the Hindus were like
plants and grass. At every juncture when the invaders
brought roaring wind followed by torrential rains, they bent
themselves and lay low. When the storm was over, they
raised their heads again and kept themselves alive and well.

Many people have accused Sir Syed Ahmad Khan of
separatism but few realize that Sir Syed was no
communalist. He was a man of liberal ideas. A picture exists
in which he is seen in the company of his Hindu friend,
Raja Jai Kishan Das, who holds Sir Syed's grandson Ross
Masud in his lap. Among the earliest contributors to his
college was a non-Muslim, Sir Mahendra Singh. His
accountant was a Hindu. He employed Hindu teachers like
J. C. Chakravartti and Pandit Shiv Shankar. He was probably
the first man in the post-1857 era to see that Britain's
success was based on modern science and technology, while
the Muslims and their supporters were defeated because
they clung to outdated and old-fashioned ideas which had
lost their utility. The Hindus had accepted the British ways
of education and social uplift, while the Muslims resisted
them. When this social progress was translated into Muslim
political language, the answer was simple democracy. But it
was forgotten in the earlier stages that in any democratic
set-up, the Muslims were bound to suffer because (a) they
were not educated in the modern art of politics, (b) they
were ill-prepared for trying this new method, and (c) they
suffered because the ratio of Hindus to Muslims was
perpetually 3:1. The majority and minority communities,
unlike in a homogenous society, were permanent and
unchangeable. Democracy, Sir Syed thought, was a game
of numbers and the Muslims were backward in it. So, for
the time being, they were supposed to bury their grievances

against the alien British and concentrate on studies and studies alone. It was more a tactic than a permanent solution.

It was at Aligarh that the third and fourth generation of students, having taken a leaf from Sir Syed's own prescription, revolted against the British and said:

Sikhaya tha tumhe nai qoum ko yeh shor o shar sara
Jo iski intiha hum hayn to iski ibtida tum ho

It is you who taught the community all this 'mischief', if we are the culminators, you are the beginner.

During the twenties and thirties the Muslims and the Hindus had come culturally closer to each other. Many had joined the anti-imperialist struggle. Muslims, in particular, showed a tendency towards Hindu-Muslim unity on the cultural front, although they were enamoured of the Muslim world, particularly Turkey. They had initially the comfortable feeling of knowing that the Hindus did nothing to whittle down their pro-Muslim tendencies. Muslims gave up eating meat, they gave money and clothes to their brethren in Turkey. Dr Ansari, the well-known physician, took a nursing mission to Turkey. It comprised men like Chaudhury Khaliquzzaman and Abdur Rehman Siddiqui—both pro-Congress at that time—who took care of the wounded Turkish soldiers. (It should be remembered that not a single Hindu went to Turkey. The Congress Press castigated Sir Syed, who was venerated by such as Mohammad Ali, Hasrat Mohani, and Zafar Ali Khan—all anti-British but all pro-Sir Syed.)

Allama Iqbal played a significant role during the earlier period in bringing the Hindus and the Muslims together. He talked of 'love' between the Hindus and the Muslims. He built a new place of worship or *Shivala* where love reigned supreme. Muslims in every province were more or less influenced by Iqbal. But there was always a movement among the Hindus that stood for reviving the bygone glories of Hinduism through *sangathan* and *shuddhi*. The Muslims, not wishing to be left behind, counter-blasted by issuing calls for *tanzim* and *ittehad* in reply to *shuddhi* and *sangathan*. It was a case of reaction against Hindu action. Iqbal's efforts to bring Hindus and Muslims closer together were soon tottering.

It must be conceded that the Hindus, due to talk of democracy, were becoming conscious of their majority. If votes were to be counted, then clearly the Hindus would be the gainers. It was natural. Hindus and Muslims were brothers all right, said Jinnah, but the difference was that while 'Brother Gandhi' had three votes, he had only one.

Hindu-Muslim Relations before the Partition of India

On the distant horizon one could see the early signs of independence for the country. It was clear that Hindus were entering a new era—the era of 'nationalism'. Revival of the national spirit, they believed, meant revival of the Hindu spirit. The natural reaction was a revival of the Muslim spirit. However, it should be noted that during this period some Hindus, particularly many Kaysthas, were still clinging to the Urdu language, which was the main cementing factor among Hindus and Muslims. Chakbast, Firaq, and Anand Narain Mullah were as respected as Akbar, Iqbal, Josh, and Jigar.

It may be mentioned here that the present writer was a student in the forties and among his classfellows in Persian was a Hindu boy. True, things were slowly changing, but some old values still persisted. Politics based on numbers was influencing every facet of life, but still the old-timers clung to the traditional methods. My private tutor was a Hindu and yet he was employed by my father, a staunch Muslim. The tutor—otherwise a good man—never failed to praise Shivaji, and directly or indirectly castigated

Aurangzeb for the latter's campaigns. He blamed Afzal Khan for using his sword against Shivaji but praised Shivaji for carrying a *punja*, or barbed five-pronged instrument that could be easily concealed in the fist. (Khafi Khan, author of *Muntakhibul Lubab*, does not mention Afzal's sword but does refer to Shivaji's *punja*). My teacher conveniently forgot to say that Hindus, Rajputs, and other warriors fought on both sides, as did Muslim soldiers during the heyday of the Mughals and before them all the rulers of Delhi.

In the old days it was more a political fight than a religious struggle. The Muslim rulers who occupied the throne were basically conquerors and only incidentally converters. They were mostly tolerant enough to allow Hindu religious practices to prosper. The mighty emperors were so powerful that they could have converted the bulk of Hindus to Islam on pain of death if they had so desired, and the whole of India would have been a Muslim-majority state, but they did not do so. This in itself is a proof of Muslim tolerance over the last eight or nine hundred years.

In the twentieth century, when Hindus began to propagate their own brand of nationalism encouraged by the foreign rulers, moderate leaders like Dadabhoy Nauroji, Gopal Krishna Gokhale, and Mohammad Ali Jinnah wanted them to go slowly and achieve freedom through joint Hindu-Muslim efforts. Combined together they could turn out the alien rulers. The Muslim leaders did not even raise objections to the use of Hindi, although Urdu was a monument to Hindu-Muslim unity. They had no quarrel with Hindu culture so long as it was confined to Hindus. They did not object to the dress, diet, art, architecture, or lifestyle of the Hindus. All they wanted was to protect the Muslim lifestyle and obtain political rights for the Muslims. Neither Sir Syed and his followers nor the other Muslim leaders raised a single point against Hindu mythology, religious practices, dress, or diet. But, more in sadness than in anger, they saw the changing attitude of the majority party. Even the Hindu historian Dr Tarachand had to concede that the cause of the division of India was more political than religious. The Hindus started eating meat and other items that were served on the Muslim *dastarkhwan*. The Muslims enjoyed the *pakoras* and *puris* which were basically part of the Hindu diet. Some Hindus put on *sherwanis*, but their distinguishing feature was their caps, (though this distinguishing feature is important). In the villages, the Hindus attended the Muslim festivals and marriages just as the Muslims participated in *Holi and Diwali* as a gesture of good will. However, in their heart of hearts the Muslims and the Hindus always treated their heroes and villains as separate entities. In my childhood we tried to avoid mentioning the controversial issues, but whenever we did, it was clear that our heroes and villains were separate: while Muslims praised men like Ghaznavi, Ghori, and Aurangzeb, the Hindus wept for Somnath and Shivaji.

Saints and Shrines

On the question of saints, *dargahs*, or religious seminars, a small percentage of Hindus was always found in attendance. Although *qawwalis* and *urs* were essentially Muslim pursuits, at least a few Hindus were always there showing respect to the holy men. I remember very distinctly that men like Justice Mulla, a Kashmiri Brahmin who was made a judge of the Allahabad High Court and was the older brother of Anand Narain Mulla, the Urdu poet, were constant visitors to the assemblage of recital of *marsia* or *majlis* organized by Muslim elders at Daryabad. Perhaps they also appreciated *marsias* (versified narrations of the valour of Hussain and the fight between the evil forces of Yazid on the one hand and Hussain on the other). Another person who commanded reverence in the forties was Sir Tej Bahadur Sapru, who usually presided over the *mushairas* and contributed to the *mushaira* fund. So did Mr (later Justice)

Gupta and Professor Amarnath Jha. Our own professor, S. C. Deb, who taught us English literature, was a personal friend of Asghar Gondvi, and while lecturing in class quoted him profusely because Urdu was the main link between Hindus and Muslims. Under the Muslim rule the predecessors of these gentlemen—commanders, governors, *vazirs,* and high dignitaries of the state—spoke to the rulers in Persian and later in Urdu. It is equally true that the Persian and Urdu of this period was an Indian version that contained words and phrases drawn from local languages, particularly Hindi. We hear the name of Abdur Rahim Khankhanah, the author of *Padmawat,* who distinguished himself as the author of the Hindi text of his versified book, but we can also cite a number of Hindu poets who wrote in Urdu and Persian.

It is remarkable that while Muslims formed the ruling class, there was rarely a time when they found themselves handicapped before Hindus because they professed a different cultural background. My own grandfather was an *ataliq* of a Hindu *jagirdar.* The *ataliq* or teacher lived in his employers' premises and taught Persian and Urdu to the sons of his employer, and on special occasions like births and marriages he wrote versified narrations praising his employer. My grandfather took pride in knowledge of the Persian and Urdu languages. And that was shortly after the turn of the century.

In the rural areas the comings and goings of the Hindus and Muslims continued, but as time passed the gulf widened because the two were distinct peoples.

Muslims Maintain a Separate Identity

India has been likened to a huge cauldron where everyone who fell into it became a part of the whole. The cauldron was forever boiling, and the foreigners who came to India and invaded this country continued to change their original language, dress, diet, and even religion and merged with those who had come earlier and lived in India. The crux of the issue is that the Muslims refused to do so and maintained their separate identity. But so long as India was ruled by the Muslims the people could afford to remain separate but loyal to the Muslim rule. The situation persisted for some time even under British rule, as evidenced by the 1857 Revolt. The Hindu sepoys fought against the British under Muslim officers. But the moment the foreigners announced that they were about to withdraw, the political separateness became clear for all to see.

Politics naturally influenced culture. Democracy, which was the order of the day, meant the game of numbers, and the Hindus were numerically large. The Muslim minority in the earlier days was ready to co-operate with the Hindus. They influenced and were also ready to be influenced, but they were not ready to merge. It can be said with historical authority that the Hindus did not see the writing on the wall. True, they had their nationalist feelings to guide them. It is also true that democracy had given them the right to revive their art, culture, and architecture. It should be borne in mind that in India the majority and minority parties were perpetual. This writer experienced this at Allahabad University, where Union elections showed that the majorities and the minorities were more or less unchanging. But democracy was also supposed to teach the Hindus that they should be tolerant of the minority point of view. It is a curious phenomenon that many religious groups were with the Hindus and were eager to co-operate with the majority community, and the Hindus felt no danger from them. Why? Because they felt they could be easily submerged and forced to hold their proper place at the bottom of society. The reason is obvious: they were less educated and had lesser understanding of the complexities of statecraft. Maulana Ashraf Ali Thanvi, who sided with Jinnah in 1938, reportedly said that statecraft was a complex subject and only Jinnah could manage it. Muslim religious groups saw politics simply in black and white. The imperialist rulers were all 'black' and the Congress was all 'white'. Little did they realize that the times had changed. The world was undergoing rapid change in the later nineteenth and twentieth centuries. It was no more a violent fight against the erstwhile supremacy. It was a constitutional struggle, and it required men with knowledge of law, modern statecraft, and a complex myriad of other issues. Urdu could hardly play a part as a common language, because the days of men like Ratan Nath Sarshar were over. The eating of meat alone could scarcely bring the two together. Culturally, for example, the Nehrus, both father and son, were close to Muslims, but not politically.

Things started changing, and changing very fast. What the Muslims had not minded or had treated as a joke a few decades earlier suddenly assumed importance. The rise of nationalism, the talk of Hindu culture, the effort to go back to Ram Raj, the revival of Hindi, the bowing before the portrait of Gandhiji, the scheme of *Vidya Mandir* and *Bande Mataram,* the treating of Muslims as *Malechhas*—these are some of the features of the time which kindled in the hearts of Muslims the same desire which had moved the Hindus. If nationalism meant the revival of the cultural mores of the Hindus, surely it applied in the same manner to Muslims. It is not surprising that the Hindus swore by nationalism and democracy, which meant Hindu nationalism and majority rule. It is natural. But what is surprising is that men like Gandhi and Nehru did not see the consequences of their stance and spurned the offer of Mr Jinnah to join hands in turning out the alien rulers. Thus politics ruled over everything in the field of culture.

Democracy, which is the ruling passion of the twentieth century, is a double-edged instrument. While it gave the Hindus the chance to act as a majority and to revive their culture and old traditions, it also opened the door to similar pursuits by the Muslims. Therefore democracy is something desirable for both in the present times.

The All-India Muslim League was, in fact, a reaction to the All-India Congress, just as Congress was a reaction to British rule. So long as cultural consciousness remained buried in the hearts, everything was rosy. But as the times progressed, the media took a step forward, and democracy encouraged a feeling of nationalism among the Hindus. Reaction was bound to follow, and the Muslims started thinking in terms of a nation. This is exactly what the times demanded. The later Soviet, African, and Asian divisions prove this point.

I do not bear any hatred for anybody but I must say that we expected too much from the changing times. As an imperialist power the British had to do what the times demanded. It would be naïve to think that they had high ideals or altruistic motives. They had none. They wished to rule as long as they could with tactics and strategies that suited them. And rule they did. The First World War weakened them so they chose to get rid of the Empire. They could see the rift—political and, naturally, cultural—between the Hindus and the Muslims which was dictated and justified by nationalism, democracy, and their own policy. The Hindus, who had remained too long under the rule of the Muslims, were influenced by 'time', democratic ideas, and the media, mostly controlled by the Hindus. They became conscious of national feelings and revived their age-old traditions, so much so that Mr Gandhi talked of Ram Raj, village economy, 'light from above', and shunned all that the West had brought. This had a visible effect on the Muslims.

The Hindus felt drawn towards *Dharma*. Naturally the Muslims were drawn towards religion and started taking their religion and culture seriously. It must be mentioned that neither the Hindus nor the Muslims were anti-religion. Akbar's *Deen Ilahi* failed miserably. The point was not lost on the Muslims that men like Abul Fazal and Sheikh Mubarak swore by that religion, while Hindus like Todar Mal—otherwise Akbar's close political ally—refused to have anything to do with it. After Akbar his new religion was dead as a dodo. So one must bear in mind that although subsequent rulers were able to make religion a matter of private worship, religious, economic, and inheritance laws were confined to Muslims, while Hindus were free to worship their own gods.

India was a continent of varied cultures which was united only by the strong unitary Government of Delhi: whoever occupied the throne, the Muslims or the British, ruled the roost. Only a strong centre kept the locals in line. By the time the British came, communications and the media had developed considerably and the warring groups were ready to co-operate, if not actually to merge. This suited the British imperial powers. Hence the existence of over 300 princely states with the British overlording them.

Things changed as the British Raj, though short-lived, initially infused a new spirit, namely nationalism, into the Hindus and the Muslims. The cultural and socio-political differences, which were hitherto hidden by the 800 years of Muslim rule, could not be brushed aside. While the provincial languages and cultures dominated, it is a fact of history that the Muslims refused to merge with the Hindus. Why? Because, in spite of their linguistic links and cultural nearness to Hindus, they still regarded themselves as Muslims. That is why the east Bengalis refused to merge with the west Bengalis. Sikhs and Hindus were closer than Sikhs and Muslims in 1947, but within less than forty years the Sikhs felt themselves a nation apart from the Hindus. Initially they inter-married and inter-dined with Hindus. At the time of partition in 1947, the Sikhs refused to shake hands with the Muslims in spite of Jinnah's pleadings. In fact the partition of the Punjab was brought about mainly because of the Sikhs. They spurned all offers by the Muslim League leader to come close to them and talk business with them. Jinnah's offer to Sikhs and Shudras was purely political but they spurned him. Once the country was divided, the Sikhs, though divided, were the main beneficiaries, but it took them only a few years to fall out with the Hindus. They decided to run separately and demanded a free country, Khalistan. The same is true of the Kashmiris. Sheikh Abdullah did his best to remain with the Hindus. The Urdu language formed a link with the Hindus, who were an educated and forward-looking minority in Kashmir, but it did not last long, and the Kashmiris too sought a separate homeland and closely associated themselves with Pakistan. Why? Because basically they were of the same stock as Pakistanis.

There is no doubt that the Khilafat Movement brought the Hindus and the Muslims closer together—so much so that the Muslims invited the Hindu leader, Gandhiji, to stand in the pulpit of the Jamia Masjid in Delhi and speak to Muslims. In their words, Muslims did their best to remain a part of the Hindus while maintaining a separate existence. But all that was temporary politics. It was not long before the Hindus and the Muslims fell apart. Khilafat *rapprochement* proved very transitory and the two major communities were soon at loggerheads. Gandhi played into the hands of the British, and Mohammad Ali's statement eschewing force against the British was published under Gandhi's secret instructions. The British policy was to keep India one. Their one hundred and fifty years rule was geared at having one army, one political system, one centre. But it was eventually broken up. The politics that divided society also divided the country. Paradoxically it was Gandhi, Nehru, Patel, and Mountbatten who divided the country into two. It was Jinnah who waited and waited to keep the country united till the end. He wanted a 'Nationalist' solution, not a Hindu-Muslim solution. Jinnah said that the Hindus and the Muslims should co-operate and defend India against an invader. In 1910, 1916, and 1946 Mr Jinnah, a nationalist in the first instance, did *not* opt for division. Under the Cabinet Mission Plan he even agreed to one Centre that would control the three essential fields: defence, currency, and foreign affairs. But the leadership of the Hindu Congress upset the applecart. It was one India as they defined it, which clearly meant domination of the majority. Muslims were not prepared to bow to that definition of India, and division was therefore the only alternative, first suggested by a Hindu leader, Lala Lajpat Rai.

The Congress leaders—who were no other than the Hindu leaders—were sure that division would fail and Pakistan would come with a begging bowl to join hands with the rest of India and then it would be treated on *their* conditions. East Pakistan broke away and they saw merit in it. Mrs Indira Gandhi said that the two-nation theory was buried deep. But East Bengal did not take the steps expected by the Indians: it did not join India. Pakistan remained alone and developed its own nationalism and strength. To join India has now become a faint hope despite local nationalisms. The best bet for the Indians, as the bigger and more organized of the two, is to give Pakistan a chance. Maybe time will force them to see the advantages in Pakistan and India coming closer, though a complete merger is at present out of the question. Treaties and friendship are still possible and desirable, but no more. No one can say what the future holds. No one is sure where India's states like Kashmir, Punjab, Assam, and the South, presently feeling restive, will eventually go. The best course for India—and for Pakistan—is to cater to the local aspirations of both. That might lead to closer co-operation and therefore contribute to world peace.

Shaista Suhrawardy Ikramullah

Born in 1915 and educated in Calcutta and London, Begum Shaista Suhrawardy Ikramullah was one of the few Muslim women to have taken part in the Pakistan Movement. She continued to play an active role in Pakistani politics in the critical, formative years of Pakistan. Later she served as Ambassador to Morocco (1964-7).

Her writings in *Ismat, Tehzeeb-e-Niswan, Humayun,* and in the magazine sections of *Dawn, The Pakistan Times, Sind Observer,* and *Morning News* established her reputation as a writer in both English and Urdu. She is the author of *Behind the Veil* (1953), *From Purdah to Parliament* (1963), and *Huseyn Shaheed Suhrawardy—A Biography* (1991). A revised and updated version of *From Purdah to Parliament* is due to be released by Oxford University Press in 1997.

Common Heritage

Shaista Suhrawardy Ikramullah

I have always believed in the importance of personal relationships and hold personal loyalty to be paramount. It has often involved me in conflict and misunderstanding but it is almost a creed with me. I believe personal friendship to be the bridge that spans the gulf of misunderstanding and distrust between nations and people. I have tried very hard, often with much difficulty, to keep this bridge unbroken.

This attitude of mine is the result of my particular upbringing and the milieu in which I grew up. I was born in a political family whose members played a significant part in the struggle for the Independence of India and the creation of Pakistan. And though from the earliest years of my childhood I cannot remember a time when my family was not involved in political struggle, still this did not affect our relationship with individual members of the community against whose domination or politics we were fighting. My father, who was a remarkable man in many ways, was also remarkable in having friends amongst every class and community. And this at a time when this was considered unusual. My earliest recollections of friends are of English children: three boys and two girls with whom my brother and I played regularly and with whom we shared the books of Beatrix Potter and Kate Greenaway. One of them is still amongst my closest friends, and the mother of one of those boys attended the wedding of my eldest daughter.

The next lot of children I remember making friends with were Hindus belonging to a very distinguished family. They were the grandchildren of Sir Surendranath Banerji, whom my father had attended during his last illness and whose daughter and son-in-law had become his very close friends; the son-in-law was the famous lawyer B.C. Chatterji.

There is an anecdote that used to amuse us very much in connection with my father's friendship with this family. They were Hindu-Brahmins and at that time, that is nearly sixty years ago, the caste rules were very strictly adhered to—it was unheard-of for a Muslim to be a houseguest or to share a meal with a Hindu family. When my father was dining with Mr and Mrs Chatterji a servant came up, seething with anger and said to Mrs Chatterji, 'Do you know what so and so is saying? that Mama is a Mussalman! I replied, "How dare you utter such a calumny, Mama a Muslim! He is a high-class Brahmin, he is Mukherji."' I think he boasted, pleased to have removed such a grave misunderstanding! Not finding the response he expected, he said: 'Wasn't I right Madam? Isn't it impertinent to call Mama a Mussalman?' Mr Chatterji replied without much enthusiasm, 'That is all right. Go along and attend to your work.' The servant went away rather abashed at not being applauded for his zeal. (My father was referred to in the traditional way as a member of the family, Mama, i.e., uncle.)

My father related this anecdote with much amusement, and he thought it very funny, but my mother was alarmed. 'You will be killed one of these days, if you go on like this,' she said. This was in 1923; tension was not so great at that date, but the communities jealously guarded their separate identities, and it was an accepted fact that for violations of the sacred taboos of either community, no punishment was great enough, but my father was far ahead in his attitude in this matter as in others. And at a time when this was not usual, if not impossible, his closest friends were English and Hindus.

Not only was he a houseguest in a prominent family like the B.C. Chatterjis, regular houseguests in our home when I was a child were a Mr and Mrs Baam, a Hindu

Maharashtra Brahmin family. When Mrs Baam got TB she came and stayed in our house to enable her to be treated by my father, and when she and her husband both died at a tragically young age, my father kept in touch with their little boy, Sunny, followed his career with interest, and his marriage was arranged by our family. To this day he remains one of our closest friends.

When I married at eighteen and went to live in New Delhi, I carried on this pattern of friendship with members of other communities. My husband's Chief was Sir Frank Noyce. In 1953 it was still most unusual for an Englishman and his subordinate to be on other than the most formal terms, but between the Noyces and us a warm friendship developed which has continued to this day. When their son Wilford Noyce, a famous mountaineer, was killed in Pamir, my husband and I grieved for him as for a younger brother. And his family and ours are carrying on this tradition of friendship.

My husband was a member of the ICS and was at that time one of the few Muslims in it. In fact he was the only Muslim ICS Officer in the Government of India. Therefore his colleagues were all English or Hindu.

If I were to recount the names of all the Hindu friends we made in this period it would make a very long list. With most of them I have been out of touch for many years, but time and distance have not dimmed the happy memories of times I spent in their company. With some of them I am still in touch. Years have passed and the tribulations that one has gone through have brought them nearer and made our friendship deeper and more valuable. They remain my closest friends, for one makes one's best friends in one's youth.

Things began to change after my return from England in 1940, after an absence of three years. The years that followed were very important. The struggle for freedom was to reach its peak and it was no longer to be a joint struggle. The demands for Pakistan as a sovereign independent state had already been formulated. With my political background it was inevitable that I should be drawn into the vortex of that struggle, and before I realized, I was in the forefront of it. I had become one of the most prominent Muslim League workers. The League was still struggling for recognition as a political party. The Quaid-i-Azam had as yet to make good his claim that there were three parties to the settlement of India's question of Independence: the British, the Hindus, and the Muslims. By temperament and tradition I have always been drawn towards lost causes, and I therefore became an ardent supporter of the Muslim League. With the thoughtlessness and audacity of youth I threw all caution to the wind, making fiery speeches, holding meetings, passing resolutions. And yet such was my naïveté that when, as a result of my activities, I began to antagonize my Hindu friends, it surprised me!

It was during the Simla Conference that I got the first shock. I had been one of the most popular members of the Women's Club known as the 'Lady Chelmsford Club', and the Secretary, a Sikh lady, was particularly fond of me. But I was told that it was she who had objected to my being invited to a party given in honour of Mrs Naidu. I could not believe it. It seemed ridiculous and incredible to me, for Mrs Naidu was like an aunt to me, a very close friend of my family. In fact, without exaggeration, there was no other member of the Club whom she knew as well as me, for she had known my parents before I was born, and not to invite me because I was a Muslim seemed too ridiculous to be true. Yet that is what happened. Mrs Naidu was equally shocked and expressed herself in her characteristic and forthright manner. She came straight to me from the Club and asked me to come with her. We went through the Mall, sitting in our respective rickshaws, talking to each other across it, to the amusement of the passers-by.

But the storm was gathering, and other clouds could not be dispelled so easily. I found myself suddenly a butt of attacks, of criticism, even of calumny. Friends dropped off, acquaintances began to shun us, the atmosphere began to be filled with hatred, distrust, and suspicion. This was 1946, and the violence was growing everywhere. The bloodbath in Calcutta was followed by others at other places, and out of this travail Pakistan was born.

Suddenly there was a gulf dividing one's former friends and making them into strangers, making what had been one's country not only an alien but an enemy territory. The changes seemed so sudden that though one had talked about it for ages, one could not accept all its implications. For instance, when I first came over from India to Pakistan I did not think of it as anything more than a transfer to another place of posting. I left my father's house in Calcutta more or less completely furnished, taking great care to see there was enough linen, silver, and china left to enable me to entertain when I came back. It was only after several months that I returned to bring with me what I could, but by that time a host of rules and regulations had made the task most difficult, so most of the things had to be left behind.

Though I did not realize it at first, one had reached the point of no return. This was brought home in so many little ways. The news of close friends became difficult to get, letters ceased to come, and those that came from relations were so cold, so lacking in warmth, giving bare family news. Months passed by, and gradually the gloom began to lighten a bit.

I remember so clearly the first letter that I received from a young Hindu friend of mine. She had written to say that she had got engaged, and sent me a photo of her fiance. Her family and we had been very close friends, and I had known her since she was a child of eight. She had grown up to be a lovely girl, and had got engaged to a boy I also knew very well. That engagement had broken, and I had been concerned about her, and now she wrote to me so say that all was well. It was heart-warming to get that testimony

of continued trust and friendship. I remember writing to
her that 'this is the bridge, my dear, that spans the river of
blood that has flowed between your country and mine. I
hope that if we keep this bridge intact we will one day
rebuild the whole edifice of friendship again.'

I began to meet former friends and colleagues in the
forum of international conferences. Some were cold and
distant, but the warmth and the affection of others like
Mrs Hannah Sen made up for it. She was a friend who had
known my family for years. When told of my activities she
said, 'Even if she breathed poison against India I'd love
her still.' I was deeply touched.

In Ottawa, in Quebec, in New York I met former friends
and went over shared memories. From 1952 to 1959 my
husband and I were posted abroad, in Canada, in France,
and then for four and half years in London. The High
Commissioner for India during that period was Mrs Pandit,
the sister of Jawaharlal Nehru. The Nehrus and our family
have had many connections and we had more or less the
same background and upbringing. And so our relationship,
to the surprise of many and I am sure to the relief of the
British Foreign Office, was extremely cordial, as it has always
been. Mrs Pandit and my husband enjoyed sharpening their
wits against each other, and the thrust and parry of their
conversation relieved the tedium of ordinary conversation
at diplomatic corps functions.

'Which language are you speaking to each other?' asked
a journalist, seeing my husband engrossed in conversation
with Mrs Pandit. 'That is the trouble,' replied my husband,
'I would call it Urdu, she would call it Hindi, and her
brother would call it Hindustani!' And in this reply in a
nut-shell was the whole problem that had resulted in the
partition of India.

At the end of our stay in London Mrs Pandit, as the
Dean of the Commonwealth Diplomatic Corps, made the
farewell speech at the dinner paying the usual compliments
to my husband that one does on such occasions. He, after

thanking her in the accepted manner, added: 'I have spent the four and a half years of my stay here telling you to take whatever Mrs Pandit says with a grain of salt. I again repeat the same.' His remark was really most apt, combining the modest disclaimer expected on such occasions with a soupçon of malice! It evoked an appropriate applause and the usual exasperated but amused remark from Mrs Pandit.

We came back home in April 1959. My husband became Foreign Secretary for the second time and India's High Commissioner in Pakistan was Mr Rajeshwar Dayal. His wife Sheila was one of my oldest friends. It was because of their personal friendship with so many prominent Pakistanis, including the President and the Foreign Minister, Mr Manzoor Qadir, that during their tenure of appointment the relationship between India and Pakistan improved to an extent it never had before or since. It was an almost miraculous proof of what personal contacts could achieve in the field. One could feel the temperature dropping and the tension lessening and the goodwill growing day by day. When Mr Brohi was appointed Pakistan's High Commissioner to India the triangle was complete. But alas! all our efforts to bring about an accord and understanding did not succeed. It is beyond the range of this article to go into the reason why the effort failed politically, but on a personal basis, the fact is that Rajeshwar Dayal was asked by Hammarskjöld to go to the Congo, and my husband fell ill and had to give up the post of the Foreign Secretary, and Brohi, left alone and isolated in his efforts, asked to be recalled.

Since then the relationship has been deteriorating and the tension mounting, to the extent of erupting into two full-scale wars. The chances of reconciliation have been severely damaged and conditions seem almost beyond repair.

As the years go by, the number of persons with shared memories on each side gets less and less. Death has claimed most of them, others have retired from the political stage.

It already seems too late for personal relationships to play any part in healing the breach, but perhaps it is not yet too late.

When negotiations took place between India and Pakistan, I hoped that personal recollections would arise and help to smooth the path—Field Marshal Mohammad Ayub Khan shared memories of army comradeship with Indian generals, while Mrs Gandhi had grown up in a household where Muslims were accepted as close family friends and she regarded many of them, and referred to them, as uncles, as is the custom in Indian households. I recall a time in 1946 when I called to see Mrs Naidu, who was staying at Mrs Gandhi's home. Mrs Gandhi brought her son Rajiv, then about two and a half years old, in her arms, and he greated us by saying *Jai Hind, Allah-o-Akbar, Inqilab Zindabad* all in one breath. In this lies the hope that the peoples of two countries which are geographically so close, and which historically have so much in common, may one day learn to live in peace and unity with each other.